Buildings for People

Buildings for People

Responsible Real Estate Development and Planning

Justin B. Hollander
Tufts University, USA

Nicole E. Stephens
Massachusetts Port Authority, USA

Contents

List of Figures

List of Tables

Author Bio

Justin B. Hollander is a professor of Urban and Environmental Policy and Planning at Tufts University and is an internationally renowned expert on the planning and design of human settlements. He co-edited the book *Urban Experience and Design: Contemporary Perspectives on Improving the Public Realm* (Routledge, 2021) and is the author of nine other books on urban planning and design. He was recently inducted as a Fellow of the American Institute of Certified Planners and hosts the Apple podcast "Cognitive Urbanism."

Nicole E. Stephens is a Development Manager for the Massachusetts Port Authority (Massport) in their Real Estate and Asset Management Department and previously worked for the Massachusetts Legislature in a variety of roles over an eight-year period. She grew up in military family housing and lived in an affordable housing unit in Boston for five years. Nicole holds a Master's in Urban and Environmental Policy and Planning from Tufts University.

Acknowledgments

Tufts students helped enormously throughout the process of researching and writing the book, including Alisha Patel, Julia Jenulis, Vicky Yang, Uma Edulbehram, Aliya Magnuson, and Myiah Webb. Special thanks go to the team at Wiley, including Todd Green, Amy Odum, and Juliet Booker. We greatly appreciate those who have granted us permission to use their images throughout the book.

Thanks to all of our colleagues at Tufts, especially Rebecca Shakespeare and Shomon Shamsuddin. Most of all, we want to thank our families for their support and love throughout the research and writing of this book.

1

An Introduction

Look around. No matter the continent, no matter the country, you will see streets, buildings, utilities, ornamental trees, manicured lawns, maybe even flowers. Some places also have bicycle lanes, trolleys, bridges, parks, or even formal gardens. As a small child might put it: how did this all get here? How are cities and towns built? Who decides and how?

Broadly speaking, this is the aim of the urban studies field to answer. In this book, we take a narrower line of inquiry by asking what the role of the real estate development and planning enterprises are in shaping how places get built and rebuilt. While a multitude of factors play into the design and development of human settlements, real estate and planning have an outsized and oft misunderstood role. The choice of where water lines are laid out, how tall a building is, what trees are planted, these each have their origins in the real estate development and planning professions – an intricate and complex set of customs, techniques, methods, theories, and histories that, situated slightly differently in different geographies reveal the answer to the child's question about the built environment.

It might be easy in telling this story to focus on a series of nameless and faceless ideas (like pro forma analysis, gentrification, or zoning) that propel the shaping and reshaping of places, but people are in fact at the center of this work – we build not because of regulations or profits or because of tradition, we build for humankind. Through this people-first lens, we will explore the practice of real estate planning and development.

The book's title "Building for People" is an homage to the seminal urban planning book *Cities for People* by Danish planner Jan Gehl (2013). Gehl can reasonably be considered the most important urban planner alive today. His work has reshaped cities globally and the impact of *Cities for People* has been profound: using psychological sciences and simple human observation, he has brought attention within the urban design and planning world to how people experience

Buildings for People: Responsible Real Estate Development and Planning, First Edition.
Justin B. Hollander and Nicole E. Stephens.
© 2023 John Wiley & Sons, Inc. Published 2023 by John Wiley & Sons, Inc.

cities (Matan and Newman 2016). Through a people-centered lens, Gehl has helped city planners make places more inviting, safer, and more accessible. We hope that this book can make a similar impact on the real estate development and planning fields.

A good deal of research has established how places affect people and how policies and stakeholders have served to produce and reinforce these effects. Understanding real estate development is a fundamental task for using this research as part of a career focused on making places better for people. While most practical guides to real estate development focus on the business side of the proposition, this book presents real estate development more holistically, elucidating the role of both profit and public good. Profit is not necessarily incompatible with social goals and this text serves as a guide to attend to financial and investment concerns, but not at the expense of social ones.[1]

This book provides an introduction to the major components of mainstream and progressive real estate development and their connections to urban planning. We will convey key technical and substantive knowledge, as well as situating the subject within a broader political, economic, and social context. Beginning with some historical and theoretical context on real estate development and planning, then moving to basic financial analysis, site selection, site improvement, architecture, landscape architecture, site planning, construction, and evaluation, this book explores key theories and methods of professional practice. We maintain a critical focus on the role of real estate in the reproduction of social, spatial, and economic inequalities and consider how alternative models function theoretically and practically in the market. We both introduce important players in the development and planning process, including urban planners, lawyers, real estate developers, bankers, community organizers, and others as well as make visible how the built environment is a reflection of the power dynamics between them. The story of real estate development and planning is told here through a multi-level lens, where the systemic factors that govern (and are governed by) the real estate process will be closely examined and interrogated, allowing you to understand how key societal trends like gentrification, affordable housing, inequality, and homelessness are intertwined with the business of real estate development and planning. Through the use of real-world examples, you will become familiar with the nomenclature and skills needed to influence and impact the physical shaping of human settlements, while understanding social, economic, and political dimensions of that work.

When you read this book, you will master new knowledge and develop new skills. This book will help you understand: (1) the historical context of real estate development, (2) what models exist to address a range of social and community goals, and (3) the basic steps of the real estate development process. Readers will master these skills: (1) ability to critically examine the real estate development and planning process, while exploring systematic factors that shape the industry, (2) determine and calculate the contextual financial and economic factors that frame any real estate development project, (3) conduct a pro forma analysis, and (4) basic site selection, site analysis, planning, design, and evaluation.

The book begins here with an overview of the history of real estate development and planning, how these two fields first professionalized, and were employed to address a range of public problems, including affordable housing. We dive deeper into these questions in Chapter 2 with an exploration of alternative models which consider the role of the public sector as collaborators in development, an Indigenous view of land, defense, and military family housing, and community development corporations (CDCs). Chapters 3 and 4 return to conventional methodologies by reviewing the capitalist perspective on real estate as a commodity, to be bought, sold, and invested in. In the subsequent five chapters, we take on each of the real estate development processes: site selection, site analysis/planning, architecture/landscape architecture, urban design and planning, and construction. For each, we review the key considerations for that process and emphasize what it means to take a people-centered approach. We also include an illustrative case study for each chapter where we examine how the lessons of the chapter come to life in the real world of professional real estate development practice. We made an effort to align the cases with each of the five development processes mentioned above, with some being true exemplars of best practices and others offering broader lessons for practice outside of a single development process. For details on our methodology for conducting these case studies, see Appendix 1.

History and Context of the Real Estate Development and Planning Process

Historically, real estate development and planning were activities that happened at all levels of society, from highly centralized monarchies looking to erect public works to individual farms wanting to build a barn. The early civilizations in Africa and Asia were renowned for their monumental structures like the Great Pyramids in Giza, Egypt that still stand today, thousands of years later (See Figures 1.1–1.3). Likewise, the decentralized building efforts of individual farmers, craftspeople, or merchants have throughout history shaped urbanized communities and continue to shape the paths of roads, locations of parks, and the structure of settlements (Reps 1965). Between those autocratic developments and the pioneers settlers of the Great Plains and the dug-out cliffs of the Anasazi people, there is a rich historical record of a middle ground of formal plans, organized platting of land, and even the equivalent of today's homeowner associations that appears to have shaped much of the planet's built environment (Platt 2014).

Figure 1.1 Example of ancient planning in the Indus Valley civilization. Archeological site of the ancient city Dholavira in modern day Gujarat, India. Courtesy of Uma Edulbehram.

Figure 1.2 Archeological site where the ancient city Dholavira once stood, in modern day Gujarat, India. Courtesy of Uma Edulbehram.

Figure 1.3 Instance of planning in Dholavira. One of 16 water baths surrounding the city perimeter that served as both storage and protection. Courtesy of Uma Edulbehram.

The choice of a despot or an independent pioneer to build or not to build is of little relevance today, but meditating on that space between offers valuable insight. When people have voluntarily come together to develop land and build, but have restricted themselves by social laws or regulations, amazing results have come: the Spanish pueblo (See Figure 1.4), the Italian plaza, the New England village, the Israeli kibbutz (See Figure 1.5), and many others.

The remainder of this chapter considers recent history in greater depth, beginning with the birth of modern urban planning and real estate development practice in the nineteenth century and major milestones in the twentieth century that brought broader public purpose with the advent in the United States of the 1949 Housing Act and subsequent federal and state legislation that sought to position the development process as a tool to solve urban and subsequently, broader societal problems. We will then discuss the historical development of alternative housing models globally, with a focus on examples in the United States and their current role in the US housing market (exploring these models in more depth in the next chapter). This review will conclude with the present-day debates around the role of real estate development and planning in shaping public and private spaces, focusing on affordable housing, gentrification, alternative models like the Yes In My BackYard movement (YIMBY).

Figure 1.4 Spanish Pueblo. ZC.Marbella / Wikimedia Commons / CC BY-SA 4.0.

Figure 1.5 Aerial view of Kibbutz Nir David near the Amal River in Israel. STOCKSTUDIO / Adobe Stock.

The Birth of Professional Real Estate and Planning in the Nineteenth Century

While we have much to learn from ancient real estate development and planning, like so many other contemporary scholars (see Hall's *Cities of Tomorrow*) we begin this historical review with the birth of modernity. It was at the dawn of the nineteenth century that humanity underwent a profound shift with the onset of the Industrial Revolution. Machines and the scientific method surely brought a lot of good to the world, but they also brought the horrors of the Great War, urbanization and its problems at a mass scale, and a wholesale rejection of many of the traditions and practices of architecture and planning of the past (Gomis and Turón 2015). In many ways, the Columbian Exposition of 1893 marked a clean break from the past and launched the birth of the urban planning profession, which was quickly followed by professionalization in scores of other cognate fields like real estate development (Fairfield 2018). Daniel Burnham and his early followers formed national professional city planning bodies in the United States and promoted model municipal regulations (See Figure 1.6).

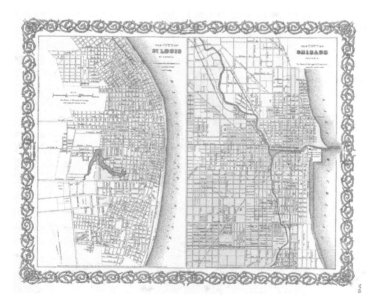

Figure 1.6 Example of professional city planning in St. Louis, Missouri and Chicago, Illinois. Hand colored maps detail city wards that demonstrate uniformity in the modern American city. J. H. Colton / Wikimedia Commons / Public domain.

While widely celebrated as a progressive advancement in the application of science and social science to solving community problems, the plainer view is that the birth of professional planning was a conduit for real estate development to acquire faster, easier, and more profitable opportunities for growth. The advent of zoning at the beginning of the twentieth century is an excellent example of this.

Zoning was first introduced ostensibly to manage the ill effects of growth, as justified in the model zoning regulations promulgated in the early 1900s (Peterson 2003). By dividing a community into zones and establishing use, density, bulk, form, and access minimums and maximums in each, the Courts generally found that zoning was a legitimate exercise of local police power (Peterson 2003). What was not explicitly argued in these seminal court cases was the invisible power of zoning in advancing the interests of real estate development. By formalizing rules of development, just about every locality in the United States and many countries around the world essentially made it much easier to grow. Sonia Hirt's (2015) *Zoned in the USA* offers a compelling comparative analysis of the ways that zoning, when used in the US, Canada, and a few other countries, removes avenues for opposition to new development projects by eliminating discretion on the part of local officials. Hirt notes that in most of the rest of the democratic world, that local discretion is preserved, and property owners (and their real estate developer partners) have few by-right opportunities to build. In North America, that right to build was enshrined by zoning. Zoning sets the ground rules for new development, which if followed precisely permits a real estate developer to be able to build. People set the rules of zoning, but once they are set in place property owners and developers have much latitude (See Figure 1.7).

Figure 1.7 1947 proposed zoning in map in Greater Winnipeg, Manitoba Canada created by municipal and state planning committees. Manitoba Historical Maps / Flickr / CC BY 2.0.

With the widespread adoption of modern planning functions like zoning, master planning, and subdivision control, the certainty of real estate development increased drastically. This led to the formation of professional real estate organizations and societies like the National Association of Realtors (1908) and the Urban Land Institute (1936). Where pre-modern era real estate development was governed by despot, a pioneer, or some collective organization in between, modern real estate is universally governed by a professional class of planners, working for locally elected political leaders in each community. These planners implement legal frameworks, like zoning mentioned earlier, that respond to the political desires of their bosses. If the people of a community want large industrial districts established on the outskirts of their downtown, then those political leaders ensure that the zoning and other regulations make that possible. Now highly professionalized by the twentieth century, real estate developers could then simply look at what is allowable by local codes and then build. (Later in the book, we will explore the creativity that tends to come along with the decision about what actually gets built.) In this context, hand-in-hand with local political leaders and professional planners, the real estate development function becomes a highly profitable business, and on an industrial-sized scale teams of financial analysts and construction experts identify allowable uses, acquire properties, build, and either lease or sell to generate profit.

Mid-twentieth Century Federal Intervention to Address Societal Problems

The end of World War II brought millions of soldiers back from the battlefield and a baby boom in America drove enormous demand for new housing. The timing coincided with the vast growth in innovation around automobile manufacturing, also a byproduct of the war (Nicolaides and Wiese 2017). With people beginning to drive more, new limited access roadways and highways being laid out, and an explosion in the number of households forming, the mid-twentieth century witnessed a wholesale transformation of the American landscape as real estate developers, working again with local leaders and professional planners, saw housing starts increase from 142,000 in 1944 to approximately 1.5 million per year by the 1950s (Nicolaides and Wiese 2017). The quintessential Levittown development on Long Island, New York was begun in 1947 and eventually consisted of 17,500 houses across 1,200 acres (Kelly 1988), followed by similar Levittowns and other comparably sized developments across the country (Beauregard 2006) (See Figure 1.8).

During this same time, discriminatory lending practices, racial zoning, and racial and religious covenants embedded in the real estate development process created unfair and unjust residential segregation across the country (Rothstein 2017). These practices will be explored in depth in Chapter 2.

Figure 1.8 Example of street in Levittown development on Long Island, New York. Library of Congress / Wikimedia Commons / Public Domain.

Federal veterans support and housing programs provided additional insurance and capital to support this building boom, with many of those programs still in effect in various forms. As previewed earlier, many of these programs were designed to largely help White families and have been criticized as discriminatory toward Black and Latino applicants (Rothstein 2017).

For those Americans lucky enough to benefit from these federal programs, innovation around lending made a big difference. One agency, the Federal Housing Administration (FHA) introduced the 30 year fixed rate mortgage, making it much easier for low to moderate income individuals to purchase a home. These FHA programs continue to be a key stimulant to residential real estate development today.

The 1949 Housing Act provided a range of federal supports for both real estate development and public housing, staking new ground in government support for intervention in the private real estate market. These programs brought a new level of public purpose to real estate development, arguing that the social and economic problems of society could be addressed through development. Here we begin to see a sense in American society that pure profit might be balanced with broader public purpose.

Upheaval in cities and growing urban poverty in the 1950s and 1960s led to further federal intervention with the 1954 Housing Act, which built upon the 1949 Act's slum clearance provisions by introducing the concept of "urban renewal" (Stafford 1976). These urban renewal programs were built on the assumption that some real estate markets fail when disinvestment and stigma are too strong and the only possible remedy is public intervention in the form of demolition and rebuilding (a rejection of that traditional Adam Smith view of the hidden hand of the market always setting prices and correcting market failures).

Across the country, federal money was and to some extent is still used by local governments to essentially condemn entire neighborhoods (always low-income and usually occupied by Black and Latino residents) and partner with real estate developers to build something new. Herbert Gans' (1965) seminal treatment of this process in Boston told the story of the West End and how it was demolished to make room for an expansion of Massachusetts General Hospital and new housing (See Figure 1.9). Gans reports on the ways that people were essentially evicted from their fully functioning homes and their personal religious, educational, and community networks were destroyed. Countless other accounts of the devastating impacts of urban renewal eventually led to its decline in popularity and increasingly more targeted use (Stafford 1976).

While these mid-century federal programs enriched many a real estate developer, they came with restrictions and limitations. The unintended consequences of urban renewal have led many scholars to question whether they were unintended in the first place (Hirsch 2000). Some have argued that the pursuit of social goals in "improving" cities was all just code for racist and discriminatory policies (Hirsch 2000). Whatever the motivation, these programs redefined the relationship between the for-profit real estate industry and the outcomes they created in building places. New real estate projects were no longer considered outside of a social and economic context.

Figure 1.9 North east view of West End urban renewal project in Boston. Boston Housing Authority / Wikimedia Commons / CC BY 2.0.

Historical Development of Alternative Housing Models

The Industrial Revolution brought more than just the professionalization of real estate and planning practice; it also brought a major wave of urbanization across the globe. In the nineteenth century, new urban slums emerged across Europe and North America, where rural migrants came pouring into packed tenements, with poor ventilation and scant natural light (Hall and Tewdwr-Jones 2010). These neighborhoods, like the Lower East Side in New York or Lombard Street in Philadelphia (Logan and Bellman 2016) were largely characterized by overcrowding, low-quality housing, poor infrastructure (water, sewerage, and electricity), and high crime (Hall and Tewdwr-Jones 2010). Photojournalist Jacob Riis (1890) is widely credited with bringing these conditions to the broader attention of the American public with his renowned *How the Other Half Lives*. In his book of photographs, Riis depicts the inhumane housing conditions among the poor in the Lower East Side of New York City (See Figure 1.10). The response was profound,

Figure 1.10   The Bandit's Roost photograph by Jacob Riis capturing urban poverty of the late nineteenth century at 59 Mulberry Street, New York City. Courtesy of the Preus Museum.

politicians responded over the coming decades by fundamentally rearranging the traditional private, for-profit real estate development model. It is not an accident that Marx (1867) wrote *Das Kapital* during this same era, critiques of capitalism were widespread and by the early twentieth century the theoretical ideas were put into practice with the Russian Revolution and the establishment of the world's first major communist state.

Within the United States, the struggle between capitalist and communist models for real estate and housing resulted in the development of many configurations which exhibited characteristics of both ideologies. Public housing became the most visible, involving the building and maintenance of subsidized homes for (at first) veterans and senior citizens, and later the poor and disabled (Vale and Freemark 2012). These twentieth century public housing developments generally replaced what was termed "slum housing," high-density, poor quality construction, but privately owned units, with modern, multi-story, homes that had a range of amenities often absent from the replaced homes, like electricity, bathrooms, running water, and sunlight (Wallace 2004) (See Figure 1.11). Over time, the lack of public support for public housing resulted in slashed budgets and disinvestment. Local public housing authorities lacked the funds, expertise, or both to adequately maintain these buildings and most fell into disrepair. As the physical plant of most public housing in America diminished, vermin, interrupted heat and hot water, and filth overwhelmed many units making these buildings housing

Figure 1.11 Slum area in early twentieth century Washington D.C. primarily housing Black residents. New York Public Library / Flickr / wikimedia Commons / Public domain.

of last resort and acceptable to only the poorest Americans (Vale and Freemark 2012). As the population of public housing became increasingly poor, crime began to rise and this intense concentration of poverty became widely scorned in popular culture and society (Freeman 2011; Harris 2018).

With the descendance of public housing in the American imagination, alternative models rose, including the subsidization of private housing. The Housing Act of 1937 first offered a provision in Section 8 of the law for federal subsidies to be used to ease the rent burden of low-income Americans, but it wasn't until the 1970s that the program gained steam in the face of declining support for public housing (Sazama 2000). Through this subsidy model, private, for-profit real estate owners could make apartments available at a discounted rate to qualified low-income residents, with the difference between the market rate and the rent received made up by the federal government (Sazama 2000).

The following chapter offers a more in-depth examination of the alternative models that have arisen in recent decades to extract greater public benefits of real estate development.

Development and Redevelopment in Shaping Affordability

When people build and rebuild places there will always be winners and losers. When a real estate developer successfully navigates the regulatory process to purchase a corn field and build a shopping center on a city's outskirts, the investors win, the developer wins, any tenants in the new building wins, and the farmer who sold the land wins. But what about others? What about the fiscal health of the community? That farmer was paying taxes, but we can expect that the sale of their land and construction of a commercial building will yield drastically higher taxes. On a five-acre farm, in a typical small Midwestern US city the farmer might pay $5,000 per year in taxes. After the land is sold and improved with buildings, roads, and other infrastructure, that tax bill could be $20,000 per year.

From the perspective of the local tax collector, this was a good project for the local government. But wait, there's more to consider. Does this new shopping center mean any additional costs to the town? In most cases, the answer is yes. The shopping center's location outside of the main center of the city may bring shoppers down largely unused streets, requiring more regular resurfacing and rebuilding of those roads (at a cost of what could be thousands per year, on average). Excessive traffic may even require the installation of new traffic lights in front of the shopping center (costing tens of thousands of dollars). Then there is the matter of the existing businesses in the downtown who now have to compete with the shopping center, if any fail, that could lead to long-term vacancy and in severe cases building foreclosure and tax delinquency. Lost revenue for the city can result from such competition, as has been widely documented when big box stores and malls locate outside of downtowns (Salkin 2005).

In sum, the net fiscal impact may still be positive for this hypothetical city, but what if the new development was housing? The costs to the local government to educate additional children can reach as high as $10,000 per pupil, with growing cities and towns needing new and expanded school buildings, new teachers, new staff, etc. Researchers have been documenting the environmental, social, and fiscal impacts of growth since the White House's first Costs of Sprawl report in 1974. From the deleterious impact on food systems to water supply to obesity rates, the kind of sprawling pattern of new growth described above has been shown to generate many losers. What becomes tricky here is that each loser only loses a marginal amount, where the winners we listed above win big.

The clearest alternative to this kind of sprawling new development is the reuse and redevelopment of existing built areas. Through the rehabilitation of historic properties or the demolition of older building and rebuilding of new structures, this approach is much more costly to the real estate developer. The greenfield site described earlier is in contrast to what might be considered a brownfield site in an existing built-up neighborhood. The US Environmental Protection Agency defined brownfields as "a property, the expansion, redevelopment, or reuse of which may be complicated by the presence or potential presence of a hazardous substance, pollutant, or contaminant" (EPA). While much of the built environment may not fall into this category, the very concept of brownfield hints at the unknowns and risks for real estate developers doing redevelopment. Rehabilitating a historic nineteenth century hospital might be a worthy endeavor, but modern hospitals have drastically different room size and floor configuration needs than they did centuries ago. Even if a new use can be imagined for an old hospital, for example housing, the conversion process is rife with uncertainties and unknowns, what conditions is the electrical wiring, how stable is the foundation, was lead-based paint used in the interior (See Figure 1.12). The questions that arise for a greenfield site are miniscule in comparison, making it naturally more attractive for any potential investors.

Urban planners have been attuned to neighborhood resistance to these kinds of redevelopment projects through a phenomenon called Not-in-my-backyard (NIMBY) (Greenberg et al. 1990). Critics of a proposed real estate development project seek to stall or cancel construction in response to elevated pollution, noise, traffic, or aesthetic impacts. In more recent decades, a counter-movement has grown that promotes new development that is viewed as beneficial to a neighborhood. These advocates embrace a play on the NIMBY acronym: Yes-in-my-backyard (YIMBY) and fight to approve real estate development projects that enhance their communities by providing housing, jobs, and environmental benefits (Lake 1993).

Figure 1.12 Suffolk County Jail in Boston, Massachusetts converted into high-end Liberty Hotel.

For redevelopment projects, whether a developer is facing NIMBYs or YIMBYs will certainly impact on their ability to successfully advance their project. In addition, there are generally higher risks in a redevelopment project that are associated with higher rewards. Redevelopment has been a feature of human settlements since antiquity, developers have always been willing to shoulder the risks of rebuilding in existing areas in exchange for higher rents and higher profits.

As with the greenfield example, a redevelopment can be a winner for the real estate developer, investors, the existing property owner, and others. Because existing, previously developed land already tends to have infrastructure, the local government costs tend to be low, making the overall fiscal impact positive for many cases (with the big exception being for residential development that may bring high numbers of new students into public schools). Often redevelopment requires some level of public support or subsidy, for example deferral of property taxes or construction of nearby parks or gardens – in which case the overall fiscal impact can be expected to be negative in the short term.

Losers in a redevelopment might be renters or commercial lessees who have enjoyed an affordable neighborhood and face the prospect of rising prices in the face of redevelopment. In a process known as gentrification, increasing redevelopment activities generate enhancements to a neighborhood through new amenities and often additional public facilities (Smith and Williams 2013).

The natural degradation of the materials that comprise structures means that, most buildings need to be completely rebuilt every 30 years (Lucy and Phillips 2000). Housing scholars describe a process called filtering where new buildings attract high rents and a high-income strata of society, where without regular maintenance and rebuilding, these buildings tend to filter to lower and lower income groups as they become increasingly less desirable (Bier 2001). Because there are such a multitude of factors that drive rent prices in any given locale, the role of filtering is somewhat ambiguous relative to other drivers.

Take the example of the North End of Boston. First platted in the 1600s, this neighborhood grew and reached its fully built out form approximately 100 years later (Goldfeld 2009). Since then, buildings have been built and rebuilt many times. Some structures have been demolished (due to fire, obsolescence, or dereliction) and new ones have replaced them, sometimes at a higher or lower density. At any given time, the relative quality of an apartment compared to others in the neighborhood will impact rents or sales price, but only to a point. The overall desirability of the North End relative to other neighborhood in Boston and the region's overall economic stature will all play a role in shaping prices.

Strolling through the neighborhood's legendary Hanover Street (See Figure 1.13), alive with Italian restaurants, bakeries, cafes, and shops, we can expect that any nearby building in need of another round of repair or rebuilding will eventually receive such investment due to the profit opportunities for doing so. Neglecting to do so would be ruinous for any property owner in the long-term.

This gentrification process, from the perspective of these property owners, can simply be the expression of their self-interest in preserving valuable real estate through its repair or rebuilding. Each individual owner, making such investments in a timetable that tends to correspond to rising demand, can over time transform

Figure 1.13 Looking northeast along Hanover Street in Boston's North End. Courtesy of Rodhullandemu, CC BY-SA 4.0. https://creativecommons.org/licenses/by-sa/4.0, via Wikimedia Commons.

a neighborhood. Such transformation has indeed occurred in the North End at least a dozen times. This cycle which enables real estate development is primarily driven by fiscal goals. During economic downturns, the incentive and ability for property owners to repair or rebuild is low, so they maintain their buildings in moderate to poor condition. When the economy goes up, along with demand for living or working in the North End, the incentive for reinvestment returns and these same owners now are motivated to make those long-delayed repairs. What had been a neighborhood of older and worn homes and offices, with concomitant low rents and low sales prices, affordable to even the poorest of the region's residents, suddenly becomes a hot market. Hence: gentrification!

The sweeping sight of cranes and construction vehicles across the neighborhood does more than increase prices for the impacted buildings, it also sends a broader message to investors that prices are going up in the North End. Such a message can then mean higher rents even for those buildings which have not been renovated, a pattern nicely documented by Harris (2018) around gentrification in Brooklyn, New York. For longtime low-income residents and businesses, the comforts of their older, worn, and, perhaps, run-down abode is now under threat – their landlord may see an opportunity for raising the rent.

This possibility of displacement is a reality for many and has been well-documented (Harris 2018). But displacement from gentrification is not universal, as Freeman (2011) showed in the gentrification of Harlem that widespread evictions were less common and that low to moderate income property owners benefited greatly from gentrification as their wealth rose with property values. While the percentage of homes in a gentrifying location that are affordable to the average income household will fall, other areas of a metropolis may become less desirable and thus offer alternate opportunities for affordable housing.

This free market system allocates people to live in certain areas, at certain times. Concerns do rise about ghettoization, both in terms of concentration of poor people or rich people in certain neighborhoods. This is an outcome the free market fails at addressing and the public and subsidized housing solutions discussed earlier offer a remedy. In fact, much of redevelopment planning focuses on neighborhood-scale local government solutions to neighborhood where market failure appears evident. For a neighborhood that might be expected to experience an infusion of investment during an economic boom time but instead continues to be overlooked by investors and abandoned by property owners, planners have used redevelopment to provide subsidies and artificial incentives for owners, have condemned poorly maintained structures and acquired them through eminent domain, and have created new special purpose government authorities to manage and streamline repair and rebuilding efforts (Dardia 1998).

Take the Carriage Town neighborhood of Flint, Michigan as an example. While a drinking water contamination crisis has made Flint well-known for public mismanagement, the city has approached reuse and redevelopment of neighborhoods in a fairly typical fashion (Hollander 2011). After decades of decline and disinvestment, the city targeted the Carriage Town neighborhood for redevelopment. While 56.9% of homes were owner-occupied (US Census Bureau 2016–2020), the remainder were landlord-owned and generally in poor condition. Today, according to a scan of renter websites, the monthly rent for a typical two-bedroom apartment in Carriage Town is about $827, where the city-wide average is $819. The redevelopment plan sought to pressure landlords to improve their properties, but demand was low and rents they were collecting barely covered taxes, water, and sewer bills. While Carriage Town benefited from city investments, our own research found that the influx of new people also changed the neighborhood's character (Hollander 2011). With the neighborhood now a reasonably attractive place to live within Flint, questions abound about how public investments were spent and what those outcomes mean for people living there and in surrounding neighborhoods that might not have seen those public dollars and attention.

The development and redevelopment process described here can vary widely from place to place, but this introduction is presented with the aim of getting you comfortable with some of the nomenclature of redevelopment, affordable housing, and gentrification, all themes we will return to regularly in this book.

Note

1 The recent growth of the impact investing field suggests that focusing on people is a broad trend in finance.

Bibliography

Beauregard, R.A. (2006). *When America Became Suburban.* University of Minnesota Press.

Bier, T. (2001). *Moving Up, Filtering Down.* Washington, DC: Brookings Institution, Center on Urban and Metropolitan Policy.

Dardia, M. (1998). *Subsidizing Redevelopment in California.* Public Policy Institute of CA.

Fairfield, J. (2018). The city beautiful movement, 1890–1920. In: *Oxford Research Encyclopedia of American History.* [online] https://oxfordre.com/americanhistory/view/10.1093/acrefore/9780199329175.001.0001/acrefore-9780199329175-e-558.

Freeman, L. (2011). *There Goes the 'Hood: Views of Gentrification from the Ground Up.* Philadelphia, PA: Temple University Press.

Gans, H. (1965). *The failure of urban renewal: a critique and some – ProQuest.* [online] www.proquest.com. https://www.proquest.com/docview/2448683604?accountid=14434 (accessed November 8, 2022).

Gehl, J. (2013). *Cities for People*. Washington, DC: Island Press.

Goldfeld, A.R. (2009). *The North End: A Brief History of Boston's Oldest Neighborhood*. History Press Library Editions.

Gomis, J. and Turón, C. (2015). Conceptual and instrumental influences in the graphic representation of urban planning: the industrial revolution and the 19th century. *Technical Geography* 10 (1): 44–50.

Greenberg, M.R., Popper, F.J., and West, B.M. (1990). The TOADS. *Urban Affairs Quarterly* 25 (3): 435–454. doi: 10.1177/004208169002500306.

Hall, P. and Tewdwr-Jones, M. (2010). *Urban and Regional Planning*. London and New York: Routledge.

Harris, B. (2018). *Making the Rent in Bed-Stuy*. New York: Amistad/HarperCollins.

Hirsch, A.R. (2000). Searching for a 'sound negro policy': a racial agenda for the housing acts of 1949 and 1954. *Undefined* [online] 11 (2): 393–441. doi: 10.1080/10511482.2000.9521372.

Hirt, S. (2015). *Zoned in the USA: The Origins and Implications of American Land-Use Regulation*. Ithaca, NY: Cornell University Press.

Hollander, J. (2011). *Sunburnt Cities: The Great Recession, Depopulation and Urban Planning in the American Sunbelt*. New York/London: Routledge.

Kelly, B.M. (1988). *The politics of house and home: implications in the built environment of Levittown Long Island – ProQuest*. [online] www.proquest.com. https://www.proquest.com/docview/303627095?pq-origsite=gscholar&fromopenview=true.

Lake, R.W. (1993). Planners' alchemy transforming NIMBY to YIMBY: rethinking NIMBY. *Journal of the American planning association* 59 (1): 87–93.

Logan, J.R. and Bellman, B. (2016). Before the Philadelphia negro: residential segregation in a nineteenth-century northern city. *Social Science History* [online] 40 (4): 683–706. doi: 10.1017/ssh.2016.27.

Lucy, W.H. and Phillips, D. (2000). *Confronting Suburban Decline: Strategic Planning for Metropolitan Renewal*. Washington, DC: Island Press.

Marx, K. (1867). *Das Capital: A Critique of Political Economy*. Volume 1, Part 1: The process of capitalist production. New York, NY: Cosimo.

Matan, A. and Newman, P. (2016). *People Cities: The Life and Legacy of Jan Gehl*. Washington, DC: Island Press.

Nicolaides, B. and Wiese, A. (2017). Suburbanization in the United States after 1945. In: *Oxford Research Encyclopedia of American History*. [online] https://oxfordre.com/americanhistory/view/10.1093/acrefore/9780199329175.001.0001/acrefore-9780199329175-e-64.

Peterson, J.A. (2003). *The Birth of City Planning in the United States, 1840–1917*. [online] *ACLS Humanities EBook*. Johns Hopkins University Press. https://hdl.handle.net/2027/heb.05838 (accessed November 8, 2022).

Platt, R.H. (2014). *Land Use and Society, Third Edition*. Washington, DC: Island Press.

Real Estate Research Corporation, White House Council on Environmental Quality (US), Urban Development. Office of Policy Development, United States. Environmental Protection Agency. Office of Planning, & Management (1974). *The Costs of Sprawl: Detailed Cost Analysis*, vol. 1. US Government Printing Office.

Reps, J.W. (1965). *The Making of Urban America: A History of City Planning in the United States*. Princeton, NJ: Princeton University Press.

Riis, J. (1890). *How the Other Half Lives*. 1890. *Reprinted in 1971*, Mineola, NY: Dover Publications.

Rothstein, R. (2017). *The Color of Law: A Forgotten History of How Our Government Segregated America*. New York and London: Liveright Publishing.

Salkin, P.E. (2005). Supersizing small town America: using regionalism to right-size big box retail. *Vermont Journal of Environmental Law* 6 (1): 48. doi: 10.2307/vermjenvilaw.6.1.48.

Sazama, G.W. (2000). Lessons from the history of affordable housing cooperatives in the United States: a case study in American affordable housing policy. *The American Journal of Economics and Sociology* [online] 59 (4): 573–608. https://www.jstor.org/stable/3487827#metadata_info_tab_contents (accessed November 8, 2022).

Smith, N. and Williams, P. (2013). *Gentrification of the City*. Routledge.

Stafford, W.W. (1976). Dilemmas of civil rights groups in developing urban strategies and changes in American Federalism, 1933–1970. *Phylon (1960-)* 37 (1): 59. doi: 10.2307/274731.

U.S. Census Bureau (2016–2020). *American Community Survey*. www.census.gov (accessed July 2, 2022).

US EPA,OLEM (2019). *Overview of EPA's Brownfields Program | US EPA*. [online] US EPA. https://www.epa.gov/brownfields/overview-epas-brownfields-program.

Vale, L.J. and Freemark, Y. (2012). From public housing to public-private housing. *Journal of the American Planning Association* 78 (4): 379–402. doi: 10.1080/01944363.2012.737985.

Wallace, D.A. (2004). *Urban Planning/My Way*. Chicago, IL: Planners Press, American Planning Association.

2

Maximizing Profit or Public Good

Profit Maximization

People choose to invest in the real estate market for different reasons. Real estate ownership can increase personal wealth through housing equity, and it can also provide financial stability with a predictable home ownership mortgage. People can actually occupy and live inside of their real estate investment (something you can't do with stocks or precious metals), sell it, or rent it – it is theirs to do with as they please. But local governments in the United States have been increasingly concerned about affordable housing and have begun to enhance the regulation of the real estate industry. In 2019, members of the Boston City Council introduced a *flipping tax* of up to 25 percent on properties over $2 million that are sold twice within a two-year period to "to stem speculation and profiteering in Boston's red-hot real estate market" (Valencia and Logan 2019). Rapid buying and selling becomes problematic when developers cater to people who seek to invest rather than live in housing units.

Real estate, specifically home ownership, can provide stability to current residents and transfer wealth to the next generation. But in the United States, there remains a dark legacy of mortgage denials to Black and other minority Americans through redlining and explicit exclusion from government-sponsored home ownership expansion programs like the GI Bill post-World War II (Rothstein 2017). Repercussions of those and other racist policies are widely felt today (Rothstein 2017). In 2016, the Federal Reserve Bank of Boston released the stunning "Color of Wealth" study, which found that Black households had a net worth of $8 compared to $247,5000 for white households (Munoz et al. 2015).

Approximately 65.5% ("Quarterly Residential Vacancies and Homeownership, Fourth Quarter 2021" 2022) of Americans own a home. Rothstein (2017)

Buildings for People: Responsible Real Estate Development and Planning, First Edition.
Justin B. Hollander and Nicole E. Stephens.

describes the policy ideals behind the US government's encouragement of ownership as, "those who owned property would be invested in the capitalist system," and the government began, "distributing pamphlets saying that it was a 'patriotic duty' to cease renting and to build a single-family unit" (ibid). Now, more than a century later, is society still encouraging real estate developers to house people and business activities or as a vehicle for people to make money? We can observe the challenge of these questions at the micro and macro levels, with individual house flippers popularized by HGTV and housing built and sold but unoccupied – often luxury dwellings. Matthew Soules (2021) described this latter phenomenon as "zombie urbanism," meaning housing units used as wealth storage, speculative assets, and second homes that are largely unoccupied for much of the year (pp. 51–52).

Zombie urbanism tends to be accompanied by economic inequality and housing instability. The *New York Post* reported in June 2021 of the resale of two condos at 220 Central Park South (See Figure 2.1) totaling $157.5 million. Each unit had previously sold for $50.9 million and for $51.4 million and were within the luxury development that holds the record for the single most expensive residential sale in the United States at $238 million (Gould 2021). A block away, the Park Savoy Hotel (See Figure 2.2) was converted into a shelter for homeless men.

The Urban Land Institute's real estate development textbook defines the public as government agencies, citizen groups, and non-government stakeholders (Miles et al. 2015, p. 123) and further outlines their roles as: collaborator, regulator, facilitator, or adversarial (p. 122). Frequently, a governing body acts as a collaborator, regulator, or facilitator while people and the public more broadly tend to be cast in an adversarial role. As a regulator, facilitator, or adversary, people and their governing bodies respond and react to proposed development as new projects are pitched. Ordinary people tend to not be centered in those processes; rather, they are an afterthought. Though, in a collaborative role, people vis-à-vis the public sector may be able to play a more meaningful role.

There are current models and periods in history in which real estate development has been something other than profit driven and more people-centered. In addition to the public sector as a collaborator in real estate development, there are three other notable people-centered rather than profit motivated development models. First, we will explore the Indigenous View of Land, specifically the Haudenosaunee's (Iroquois') Seventh Generation Principle and how that ethos is expressed by different tribes and their land use decisions historically and into the present day. Secondly, we will detail Defense

Figure 2.1 Exterior view of 220 Central Park South in New York City. GrissJr / Wikimedia Commons / CC BY-SA 4.0.

and Military Family Housing and how in the late 1930s and early '40s, as the United States expanded its military and industrial capabilities, there came an acute need to house those workers and their families. We will explore the tension between desires to maintain local control and the pressing and immediate needs of that workforce. Finally, with community development corporations (CDCs), we will examine how they have developed over the past fifty years in response to a perceived failure by the government and private entities to provide needed affordable housing.

Figure 2.2 The converted Park Savoy Hotel on 58th Street in New York City. Jim. henderson / Wikimedia Commons / CC BY-SA 4.0.

The Public as Collaborators

The public/private partnership model, also referred to as P3 projects, is one approach to centering people in development projects (Miles p. 159). These projects tend to constitute a local government body as a landowner seeking a private entity to develop a land parcel for a specific purpose – Public Land Development (PLD) (Singhapathirana et al. 2022).

In their international review of PLD, researchers Singhapathirana, Hui, and Jayantha identified thirty-eight critical factors for successful PLD and categorized them broadly into eleven factors:

1) Land Allocation Strategy
2) Revenue Generation and Managing Financial Risk
3) **Delivery of Housing and Public Infrastructure**

4) Balance between Profit Generation and Accountability
5) Local Agent(s) with Devolved Power and their Interests
6) Institutional Rules and Procedures
7) Inter and Intra Agency Coordination
8) Politic and Power Relations
9) Integration of Land Development and Spatial Planning
10) Managing Unauthorized Uses and Resettlement
11) Land I.nformation Management (p. 5, 6)

Of particular interest to this book are the critical factors the researchers identified under the "Delivery of Housing and Public Infrastructure" category. Those factors include:

i) Provision of social housing and affordable housing
ii) Provision of public infrastructure
iii) Maintaining a housing mix
iv) Land-based infrastructure financing system (ibid)

Decades prior to this review, Simmons, in his 1994 paper *Public Real Estate Management and the Planner's Role*, called for the creation of a specialized field, "that focuses on skills and policy issues related to managing public development and public real estate" to bridge the gap between public and private developers (p. 334). Still, the United States is dominated by a market-led development ideology in comparison to state-led developments in China, the Netherlands, Sweden, and Finland (Singhapathirana et al. 2022, pp. 3–5). Public lands, consisting of federal and state-owned parcels, constitute 39% of total land area in the United States (See Figure 2.3) and are used primarily for recreation, forest and wildlife services, and profit generation from timber harvesting and gas drilling (ibid p. 4). The recreational and forest/wildlife services are very much people-centered uses of public land while the latter profit-motivated land uses tend to serve for-profit activities. Using land to generate profit stands in contrast to the sustainable land uses and philosophies of the native tribes in North America what we turn to next.

Indigenous View of Land

In the United States, many of the laws and practices regarding land use and property rights derived from extractive and colonial roots, grounded in the philosophical works of British men like John Locke and Adam Smith and their views of government and property (Freyfogle 2006a). The abundance of unpopulated and underutilized land (in the mind's eye of early Americans) along with the free market viewpoint only hardened with westward expansion and highly contested concepts like manifest destiny. Prior to the Revolutionary War when he was a map

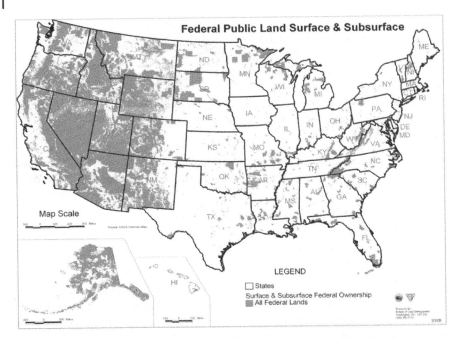

Figure 2.3 Federally controlled land as of 2005. United States Bureau of Land Management.

maker, George Washington and others surveyed and awarded land in 1774 in what is now known as West Virginia along the Kanawha River (See Figure 2.4) to veterans of the French and Indian War (Washington et al. 1774). At the time of the map's creation, the land was used by the Iroquois, Lenape (Delaware), and Shawnee people for hunting (Knollinger 2019). But the land uses by these native peoples and others were not respected or valued as the most productive and highest use. They and other Indigenous peoples had a quite different relationship with land and land use than the colonists.

The colonists and subsequent US law reflect a Western attitude that values private singular ownership over communal or even public ownership. The scholar, Freyfogle in 2006 described private property "as one of the central pillars of American society ... also, a check on state power in that it protects the individual against an overreaching state" (Freyfogle 2006a, p. 4). Contrastingly, the researchers Singhapathirana, Hui, and Jayantha found that African countries like Kenya and Botswana "provide evidence on legal pluralism in land tenure" (2022, p. 4).

Indigenous peoples have a unique relationship to land. While not uniform, it can be viewed generally as antithetical to United States and Western thought. Bob Joseph, a Gwawaenuk Nation member, provides trainings and resources for

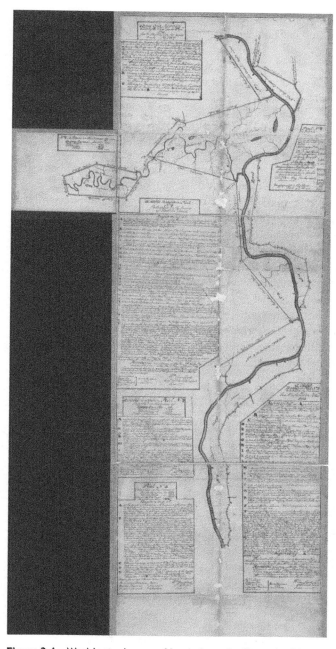

Figure 2.4 Washington's map of land along the Kanawha River. Library of Congress, Geography, and Map Division.

people to better understand, work with, and respect Indigenous peoples. He describes the general difference between the Indigenous and Western view of land as such:

> (I)[Indigenous] The land is sacred and usually given by a creator or supreme being.
>
> (W)[Western] The land and its resources should be available for development and extraction for the benefit of humans (Joseph n.d.).

To the Haudenosaunee people (also known as the Iroquois), this was embodied in the Seventh Generation Principle, in which decisions made today (in land, water, relationships, etc.) should be sustainable for the next seven generations, which is roughly 140 years (NativeKnot.com 2019; Engle et al. 2022).

These dialectic views toward land played out in the Plains of the Midwest. Many native tribes were nomadic and would move throughout the land rather than erecting permanent dwellings like those of European colonists. Certain places on the Plains were sacred. Native tribes buried the dead and maintained a connection with their ancestors on sacred land. The Black Hills (See Figure 2.5) were sacred land to the Lakota, Cheyenne, Omaha, Arapaho, Kiowa, and Kiowa-Apache peoples ("Black Hills – Stories of the Sacred" 2012). The United States government recognized this connection to the land in the Fort Laramie Treaty of 1868. The government set aside reservation land for the Lakota people, who were

Figure 2.5 Needles Highway in the Black Hills of South Dakota. Runner 1928 / Wikimedia Commons / CC BY-SA 4.0.

referred to as the Sioux by their enemies (Black Hills Visitor 2017), in the Black Hills and banned settlers from that area ("Black Hills – Stories of the Sacred" 2012). That is, until gold was discovered.

The discovery of gold in the sacred Black Hills and continued fighting between the Native peoples and the US Army led the federal government to seize the land in 1877 from the Lakota. More than a hundred years later, the US Supreme Court in *United States v. Sioux Nation of Indians* ruled that the land had been seized without just compensation and offered the tribe pecuniary compensation in the millions. The Lakota tribe rejected this money and still maintains their right to the land. Reporter Frederick Frommer interviewed Holy Rock a former tribal leader. In describing the tribe's continued refusal of the settlement, Holy Rock, asserted, "We have a different set of values ... we don't think of the air and water in terms of dollars and cents" (Frommer 2001). The settlement money ordered by the US Supreme Court is still accruing compound interest.

There is further history of the government forcing Indigenous peoples to adopt Western/colonial land use and development practices with the *General Allotment Act of 1887*, also referred to as the *Dawes Act*. Under this federal program, the native nations were stripped of their communal land holdings and decision-making power and ownership was devolved to individual members of the tribe in small parcels meant for personal use (Chang 2011).

> White U.S. citizens who wished to obtain Indian lands for their use or speculation voiced support for allotment, but the immediate impetus for the program came from Anglo-American reformers dedicated to liberalism and to the colonial mission to 'civilize' the Indians...by breaking up tribal lands, they hoped to weaken tribal bonds. By nurturing individual landownership, they hoped to cultivate economic individualism.
>
> (ibid p. 109)

Describing these disparate views, Fraley (2007) wrote:

> there is a distinct preference for individual rights over communal ones. When Native Americans described land as 'owned by everyone' what the American legal system decided was that the land was 'owned by no one.' Collective rights effectively 'do not translate into U.S. law.
>
> (p. 120)

The allotment policy was widely used in what was set aside as permanent Native land in Oklahoma and, over subsequent years enabled the selling of land to non-Natives. Much of the land became owned by white settlers, a later factor in Oklahoma's push for statehood.

A newer iteration of allotment, the 1971 law Alaska Native Claims Settlement Act (ANCSA), created new for-profit Native corporations to hold land titles and develop on behalf of their members (called shareholders) rather than tribal governments. Ganapathy (2011) detailed a failed land swap in the Yukon Flats region (See Figure 2.6) between the Native corporation Doyon and the US Fish and Wildlife Service, in which Doyon wanted to pursue oil and gas development. While most of the shareholders are Alaskan Native, Ganapathy estimated that about 25% of them live near or on land that would be directly impacted by any resource development (p. 4). Ganapathy noted contrasting opinions from shareholders at a public meeting. One testifying to maintain "subsistence practices like fishing and moose hunting" (pp. 10–11) and expressing disillusionment with the idea that they and their children would benefit from any development. Another testified, expressing hope that Doyon as a Native corporation would do it the "proper way" and "for the sake of future generations" (p. 11). The land swap was

Figure 2.6 Yukon Flats National Wildlife Refuge in Alaska. Heuer, Ted / Wikimedia Commons / Public domain

unsuccessful due to environmental concerns and mounting objections from Native Alaskans.

In the summer of 2020, the US Supreme Court ruled in *McGirt v. Oklahoma* that much of Oklahoma was under the jurisdiction of various tribal nations rather than the state. While this decision was limited to court proceedings and the state of Oklahoma is arguing for the Supreme Court to review the decision, it does indicate an evolution of federal policy in recognition of Indigenous peoples and their governing apparatuses (Wamsley 2020; Gowen and Barnes 2021; Rubin 2021). While that case did not give land title or development rights back to the Native people, it acknowledged that they had the authority over how laws and justice were carried out on that land.

Also reflecting this shift in Western attitudes but going even further, in 2003 the Federal Court of Canada returned to the Squamish Nation control of about 10 of their original 80 acres of reservation land in downtown Vancouver. In contrast to the Native corporation process in Alaska, the members of the tribe were asked to vote on the proposed development of the land. With over 80% in approval, the Squamish Nation broke ground this past fall on Señákw (See Figures 2.7–2.10), a development that will be net zero and will consist of 11 towers and about 6,000 units of housing (Chan 2019; Sterritt 2019; Halliday 2020).

US laws continue to favor private property, individual ownership, and land use. The importance of being people-centered though, may be shifting toward a more holistic view reminiscent of the Native inhabitants of America rather than the settlers, with many developments focusing on sustainability. With increased awareness and teaching of concepts like the "Racial Wealth Gap" (Munoz et al. 2015)

Figure 2.7   Close-up of towers in proposed *Señákw* development, from urban perspective. Courtesy of Revery Architecture.

Figure 2.8 Aerial view of *Sen̓áḵw* development. Courtesy of Revery Architecture.

Figure 2.9 Context of *Sen̓áḵw* development within Greater Vancouver, Canada metropolitan area. Courtesy of Revery Architecture.

and "Redlining" (Rothstein 2017) and the US government's racist lending and housing discrimination policies (Engle et al. 2022). Broader ecological, social, and climate challenges are also forcing a reexamination of land policies and how they affect communities in contrast to the centering of an immediate and individual person or even a nation-state's gain. Government's role in land management, use, and real estate development continues to evolve, reflecting shifting attitudes and norms.

Figure 2.10 Close-up of towers in proposed Seńáḵw development, from park/nature perspective. Courtesy of Revery Architecture.

Defense and Military Family Housing

The twentieth century in America saw an evolution of government's role in development, as briefly described in Chapter 1. Zoning policies began to be implemented at the local level at the beginning of the twentieth century and, as a part of President Roosevelt's New Deal, housing production became an action of the federal government. Stemming from progressive movements in the United States and abroad, the Federal Housing Administration (FHA) and Works Progress Administration (WPA) sought to put people to work in the construction industry, address housing shortages near industrial centers, and provide financing for home ownership (Kotval 2003; Wilson 2015). Through this, the United States began experimenting with public housing as well.

This trend of government involvement in housing production only accelerated as war engulfed the world in the 1930s and '40s. Industrial centers expanded and converted to military production through the entrepreneurship of firms. These workers and their families needed a place to live as they relocated near job centers. It was estimated that there was a gap of roughly 200,000 housing units for these war effort workers (Wade 1980, p. 358). Formally, the Lanham Act of 1940 saw direct legislation and funding to authorize "defense housing" as well as expanded military family housing for members of the armed forces (Kotval 2003; Peterson 2013; Reft 2015; Wilson 2015). The government sponsored the development of housing near strategic industrial centers and on military installations.

The federal government's housing goals did not always align well with local political interests. The renowned architect Frank Lloyd Wright was contracted to design housing for defense workers in Pittsfield, Massachusetts. He called his unique design "Cloverleaf Housing" (Kotval 2003; Levulis 2014). Each cluster would contain four units with two shared walls at the center to bear most of the utilities, and each unit within the cluster would have its own garage, roof deck, and yard (Levulis 2014) (See Figure 2.11).

Wright met powerful resistance in Massachusetts Congressman John McCormack (then Majority Leader but future Speaker of the US House of Representatives) and other politicians who "saw more merit in employing local architects than encouraging good design" (Kotval 2003, p. 26). In addition to politicians, real estate and banking industries opposed the new federal role in housing. They believed it would depress real estate values and sought to limit and constrain any program (Kotval 2003, p. 29; Reft 2015). In the case of Cloverleaf Housing in Pittsfield, none were built, and Wright was removed from the project. A more traditional-looking subdivision designed by local architects was ultimately built and after the war it became a part of the Pittsfield Housing Authority before it was ultimately demolished and replaced by fifty new affordable single-family homes in 1970 (Kotval 2003; Levulis 2014).

On the West Coast, the US Navy created new housing for military families and defense workers. Thousands of units were built on the Kearny Mesa plateau and became known as Linda Vista in 1941 (Monteagudo 2021). Much of the same tension between local and federal interests played out in southern California,

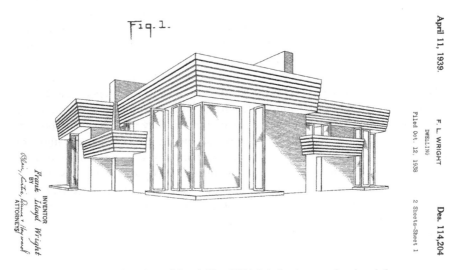

Figure 2.11 Perspective view of Frank Lloyd Wright's Suntop quadruplex defense housing.

with local real estate interests particularly frustrated initially (Reft 2015). After World War II, those interests successfully lobbied that the homes in Linda Vista be privatized. Debates emerged over who should be given priority in purchasing the units: current residents, military members, veterans, or defense workers. There were even evictions of higher-income residents; but by 1956, all the housing units were privately owned (Reft 2015).

Following the mixed results of government's role in housing and development from that time and reflecting broader trends in the role of government, government receded from building physical housing. The 1970s and 1980s saw the creation of Section 8 housing vouchers and the low-income housing tax credit (LIHTC), which incentivized the private market to accept low-income tenants or to build affordable housing (as we introduced in Chapter 1). The government moved to fund housing development rather than building it themselves. In some areas, the private market's attempt to address housing needs were inadequate.

Community Development Corporations (CDCs)

In contrast to private and government developers, community development corporations (CDCs) are community-based non-profits that develop housing and businesses and provide services, programs, and additional aid to revitalize the neighborhoods they serve (Gittell and Wilder 1999; Frisch and Servon 2006). CDCs started in the 1960s and are funded by donations or grants from the government or charitable foundations. Some of the first CDCs were funded through the Ford Foundation, a charity created by the founders of Ford Motor Company (Gittell and Wilder 1999). CDCs are often associated with affordable housing creation and preservation in urban areas, especially in minority communities. In Massachusetts, there are more than sixty certified CDCs, including the Asian Community Development Corporation (ACDC) based out of Boston's Chinatown neighborhood (The Massachusetts Association of Community Development Corporations (MACDC) n.d.).

Boston's Chinatown (See Figure 2.12) has faced many challenges. The neighborhood was a part of Boston's wave of urban renewal and "slum clearance" in the 1950s. The 1960s saw highway expansion, with I-90 to the south and I-93 to the east, hem in the neighborhood, and it was further hemmed in by the Tufts medical facility expansion within and bordering the neighborhood (Lai et al. 2001). The city of Boston seized land in 1965 to enable the expansion of the Tufts medical facility, then called Tufts – New England Medical Center T-NEMC (ibid, p.4). Additionally, Boston's "combat zone" was a sanctioned area of adult and explicit stores and businesses in the 1960s and '70s along the western edge of the neighborhood on Washington Street (ibid).

Figure 2.12 Boston Chinatown's historic entrance. Inscription on gate is from Sun Yat Sen's calligraphy "天下為公" (Everything under the sun for the public). By Ingfbruno / Wikimedia Commons / CC BY-SA 3.0.

The 1980s saw private real estate development and interest return and grow in Boston's downtown, including Chinatown. In 1987, ACDC was established to create and preserve affordable housing in Chinatown for families in response to this city resurgence. The neighborhood continues to face pressures from luxury real estate development, speculation, and, more recently, short-term rentals popularized by Airbnb (Conti 2017; Hung 2018a, 2018b).

ACDC has built over 375 low to moderate income housing units in the region. ACDC teaches a first-time home buyer class in English and Chinese, and builds community through its youth programs and "placekeeping" activities for the Asian American community ("Affordable Housing" n.d.). Their mission has evolved over the years as the organization has expanded the number of housing units, the complexity of the developments, and even the service area to Asian communities in Malden, north of Boston, and Quincy in the south.

ACDC developed an "ANCHOR" strategy to preserve community areas: **A**ctivation, **N**eeds, **C**ommunity, **H**ousing, **O**pen spaces, and **R**esidents ("Introducing ANCHOR: ACDC's Creative Placemaking Initiative" 2018). One such area is their 66 Hudson at One Greenway development in 2015, a 363 unit mixed-income development with affordable ownership opportunities, located on what had been known as Parcel C (McCafferty 2015). Parcel C had been seized and leveled for urban renewal in the late 1950s. In the '60s after it was cleared of residents, it was left vacant and underdeveloped, promised for community use, then slated for a massive parking garage, before finally being returned to the Chinatown community in 1994 (Lai et al. 2001). In addition to housing, the Greenway development includes the Pao Arts Center, retail space, and open space. The open space is frequently used for placekeeping activities like encompass bench and gazebo, see Figures 2.13–2.14, designed by Gianna Stewart with three inward facing chair swings that are embellished with stories from the neighborhood ("Hudson Street Stoop" n.d.). Non-profit

Figure 2.13   Photos of ACDC's Storytell & Sway. Photo by Nicole Stephens.

Figure 2.14   Photos of ACDC's Storytell & Sway. Photo by Nicole Stephens.

developers like ACDC, play a vital role in housing preservation and creation by filling needs that are unmet by private, profit motivated developers.

Alternative Models Summary

With the history from Chapter 1 and this chapter's examination of an array of alternative models of real estate development that are people-centered, we can now present a clearer portrait of what we mean when we say "people-centered development" (see Figure 2.15). First, affordable housing is concerned with housing people at a variety of income levels rather than chasing the greatest profit. Next, the secondary tier includes community driven amenities which can identified by the pre-existing community and are not meant to garner profits for the developer. Non-profits and new small businesses often struggle to find space to operate and ideally would fill these kind of amenity spaces. Access to public transportation is essential in people-centered development because it does not assume that a resident has access to a personal vehicle. Finally, outdoor space is increasingly becoming privatized and monetized. But, in people-centered development, rather than the outdoor space be an amenity for the residents only, the existing community is invited to enjoy the space as well.

Government plays a powerful role either directly with public land or indirectly with financing. Government can require or incentivize development patterns and practices; one such thing is the role of profit in development. Should sustainability and the benefits in seven generations be considered? Whose benefit matters more, an individual's profit or a community's need? At the tertiary tier, profit in people-centered development is possible, but only after primary and secondary needs are met. Non-profits already operate under this mindset; what profit is made is

Figure 2.15 People-Centered developments. By Nicole Stephens.

redirected into the community that they serve. We will further explore the role of profit in the following chapter and in the case studies that follow, while also highlighting other key people-centered development characteristics.

Bibliography

Affordable housing. (n.d.). Asian Community Development Corporation. https://asiancdc.org/affordable-housing (accessed November 26, 2021).

Black hills – stories of the sacred. (2012). Indigenous Religious Traditions, November 18, 2012. https://sites.coloradocollege.edu/indigenoustraditions/sacred-lands/the-black-hills-the-stories-of-the-sacred.

Black Hills Visitor (2017). Lakota or Sioux? September 6, 2017. https://blackhillsvisitor.com/learn/lakota-or-sioux.

Chan, K. (2019). Squamish nation approves 6,000-home Senakw development in Vancouver. *Urbanized*, December 11, 2019. https://dailyhive.com/vancouver/senakw-vancouver-approved-squamish-first-nation-westbank.

Chang, D.A. (2011). Enclosures of land and sovereignty: the allotment of American Indian lands. *Radical History Review* 2011 (109): 108–119. doi: 10.1215/01636545-2010-018.

Conti, K. (2017). Activists March against Airbnb Rentals They Say Are Squeezing Chinatown. *The Boston Globe.* October 5.

Engle, J., Agyeman, J., and Chung-Tiam-Fook, T. (2022). *Sacred Civics.* London: Routledge. doi: 10.4324/9781003199816.

Fraley, J.M. (2007). Reparations, social reconciliation, and the significance of place: a legal and philosophical examination of indigenous cases in the United States and their global implications. *Humanity & Society* 31 (1): 108–122. doi: 10.1177/016059760703100107.

Freyfogle, E.T. (2006a). Goodbye to the public-private divide. *Environmental Law* 36 (1): 7–24. https://www.jstor.org/stable/43267243.

Frisch, M. and Servon, L.J. (2006). CDCs and the changing context for urban community development: a review of the field and the environment. *Community Development* 37 (4): 88–108. doi: 10.1080/15575330609490197.

Frommer, F.J. (2001). Sioux Indians want land, not millions. *Washington Post,* October 14, 2001. https://www.washingtonpost.com/archive/politics/2001/10/14/sioux-indians-want-land-not-millions/0697e1e8-bf01-4ca5-9bd7-5abd63e5cfc0.

Ganapathy, S. (2011). Alaskan neo-liberalism: conservation, development, and native land rights. *Social Analysis* 55 (1): 113–134. doi: 10.3167/sa.2011.550106.

Gittell, R. and Wilder, M. (1999). Community development corporations: critical factors that influence success. *Journal of Urban Affairs* 21 (3): 341–361. doi: 10.1111/0735-2166.00021.

Gould, J. 2021. NYC condos sell for $157.5M—one block from homeless shelter. *New York Post*, June 9, 2021. https://nypost.com/2021/06/09/nyc-condo-sells-for-157-5m-a-block-from-homeless-shelter.

Gowen, A. and Barnes, R. (2021). Oklahoma reels after supreme court ruling on Indian tribes. *The Seattle Times*, July 24, 2021, sec. Nation & World. https://www.seattletimes.com/nation-world/oklahoma-reels-after-supreme-court-ruling-on-indian-tribes.

Halliday, M. (2020). The bold new plan for an indigenous-led development in Vancouver. *The Guardian*, January 3, 2020. sec. Cities. https://www.theguardian.com/cities/2020/jan/03/the-bold-new-plan-for-an-indigenous-led-development-in-vancouver.

Hudson street stoop. (n.d.). *Asian Community Development Corporation*. https://asiancdc.org/hss (accessed 9 April 2022).

Hung, M. (2018a). As Airbnb moves in, Boston's Chinatown sees its culture—and demographics—change. *Pacific Standard*, March 29, 2018. https://psmag.com/economics/airbnb-boston-chinatown-culture-demographics-change.

———. (2018b). Luxury Developments, Gentrification, Airbnb: The Battle For Boston's Chinatown. *HuffPost*, November 15, 2018, sec. Impact.

Introducing ANCHOR: ACDC's creative placemaking initiative. (2018). *Asian Community Development Corporation (blog)*, October 4, 2018. https://asiancdc.org/blog/2018/8/30/introducing-anchor-acdcs-creative-placemaking-initiative-dwazh.

Joseph, B. (n.d.). *Indigenous peoples worldviews vs western worldviews*. https://www.ictinc.ca/blog/indigenous-peoples-worldviews-vs-western-worldviews (accessed November 5, 2021).

Knollinger, C. (2019). Wild, Wondering West Virginia: Exploring West Virginia's Native American History. *West Virginia Public Broadcasting (WVPB)*, February 8, 2019, sec. WVPB News.

Kotval, Z. (2003). Opportunity lost: a clash between politics, planning, and design in defense housing for Pittsfield, Massachusetts. *Journal of Planning History* 2 (1): 25–46. doi: 10.1177/1538513202239695.

Lai, Z., Leong, A., Wu, C.C., and Kang, J. (2001). *The Lessons of the Parcel C Struggle: Reflections on Community Lawyering: Boston Chinatown*. Los Angeles: Leadership Education for Asian Pacifics: University of California Los Angeles Asian American Studies Center.

Levulis, J. (2014). Frank Lloyd Wright and Pittsfield: what could've been. *WAMC Northeast Public Radio*. https://www.wamc.org/new-england-news/2014-10-24/frank-lloyd-wright-and-pittsfield-what-couldve-been.

McCafferty, N. (2015). *Chinatown celebrates new apartments*. December 4, 2015. https://www.mhp.net/news/2015/chinatown-celebrates-new-apartments.

Miles, M.E., Netherton, L.M., and Schmitz, A. (eds.) (2015). *Real Estate Development: Principles and Process*, 5e. Washington, DC: Urban Land Institute.

Monteagudo, M. (2021). From the archives: Linda Vista started with a housing boom in 1941. *San Diego Union-Tribune*, March 23, 2021, sec. Local History. https://www.sandiegouniontribune.com/news/local-history/story/2021-03-23/from-the-archives-linda-vista-housing-1941.

Munoz, A.P., Kim, M., Chang, M. et al. (2015). *The color of wealth in Boston*. SSRN Scholarly Paper ID 2630261. Rochester, NY: Social Science Research Network. doi: 10.2139/ssrn.2630261.

Peterson, S.J. (2013). *Planning the Home Front: Building Bombers and Communities at Willow Run. Historical Studies of Urban America.* Chicago: University of Chicago Press.

Quarterly residential vacancies and homeownership, fourth quarter 2021. (2022). *United States Census Bureau.* https://www.census.gov/housing/hvs/files/currenthvspress.pdf.

Reft, R. (2015). The privatization of military family housing in Linda Vista, 1944–1956. *California History* 92 (1): 53–72. doi: 10.1525/ch.2015.92.1.53.

Reft, R. (2017). The Metropolitan Military: Homeownership Resistance to Military Family Housing in Southern California, 1979–1990. *Journal of Urban History* 43 (5): 767–794. doi.org/10.1177/0096144215590582

Rothstein, R. (2017). *The Color of Law: A Forgotten History of How Our Government Segregated America.* Liveright.

Rubin, J. (2021). *Oklahoma asks high court to nix landmark tribal-land ruling (1).* August 9, 2021. https://news.bloomberglaw.com/us-law-week/oklahoma-aims-for-barretts-vote-to-nix-landmark-tribal-ruling.

Singhapathirana, P.I., Hui, E.C.M., and Jayantha, W.M. (2022). Critical factors affecting the public land development: a systematic review and thematic synthesis. *Land Use Policy* 117 (June): 106077. doi: 10.1016/j.landusepol.2022.106077.

Soules, M. (2021). *Icebergs, Zombies, and the Ultra Thin: Architecture and Capitalism in the Twenty-First Century,* 1e. New York: Princeton Architectural Press.

Sterritt, A. (2019). Squamish nation in B.C. votes yes to develop housing mega-project on its land | CBC News. *CBC*, December 11, 2019. https://www.cbc.ca/news/canada/british-columbia/squamish-nation-votes-yes-to-develop-mega-project-on-their-land-1.5391554.

The Massachusetts Association of Community Development Corporations (MACDC) (n.d.). *Certified CDCs.* https://www.macdc.org/certified-cdcs (accessed April 20, 2022).

Valencia, M.J. and Logan, T. (2019). Boston officials propose new taxes on some real estate deals to pay for more housing. *Boston Globe*, January 13, 2019. https://www.bostonglobe.com/metro/2019/01/13/amid-housing-crunch-city-officials-propose-new-real-estate-taxes-flipping-and-sales-over-million/XJZYMQuftehY9I2ATdBYqM/story.html.

Wade, M.G. (1980). *David Reichard Williams: Avant-Garde Architect and Community Planner, 1890–1962.* Ann Arbor, MI: University Microfilms International.

Wamsley, L. (2020). Supreme Court rules that about half of Oklahoma is Native American land. *NPR*, July 9, 2020, sec. Law. https://www.npr.org/2020/07/09/889562040/supreme-court-rules-that-about-half-of-oklahoma-is-indian-land.

Washington, G., Lewis, S., and Crawford, W. (1774). *Eight survey tracts along the Kanawha River, W.Va. showing land granted to George Washington and others.* [?, 1774] Map. https://www.loc.gov/item/75693268.

Wilson, B.B. (2015). Before the 'triple bottom line': new deal defense housing as proto-sustainability. *Journal of Planning History* 14 (1): 4–18. doi: 10.1177/1538513214529404.

3

Just Another Class of Investment

Basic Financials

Any book on real estate development needs to offer some broader context before delving into the subject at hand. The previous two chapters offered some background, some introduction to the history of real estate development and planning, and an overview of some of the themes that will be explored in more detail in these chapters. In the North End example from Chapter 1, we hoped to impress upon the reader that real estate development is driven primarily by money. To understand development means being able to answer this question: can a property owner afford to make improvements and recoup those through rents or a sale. If many owners cannot afford improvements, public intervention and support is necessary for change. Urban planning comes into the equation in two ways. First, to enhance the property owner's investment choices – relaxing regulatory burdens to maximize an owner's profits and property values, subsidizing rehabilitation or renovation projects, or adjusting use requirements to invite a range of profit-making uses on a property. Second, urban planners also maintain broader order, efficiency, and community standards (tools like zoning can forbid noxious uses like slaughterhouses in close proximity to housing), altogether contributing to stability. Third, when markets fail and public intervention is needed, planning can help bring community leaders and property owners together through government-supported urban redevelopment.

For the first time in this book, we see how the twin topics here, real estate development and planning, are inextricably linked. Real estate developers need planners to execute both of those roles just mentioned. Planners cannot do anything without real estate developers working in partnership with property owners (or where they themselves are property owners). These planning and development functions are quite different, planning is inherently governmental, tending toward bureaucratic, where real estate development is primarily private, largely for-profit, and tend toward entrepreneurial and free-spirited. The public and governmental dimensions of planning will be examined in detail through the

Buildings for People: Responsible Real Estate Development and Planning, First Edition.
Justin B. Hollander and Nicole E. Stephens.
© 2023 John Wiley & Sons, Inc. Published 2023 by John Wiley & Sons, Inc.

following chapters. It is the profit-motivating dimension of real estate developers that demands additional treatment here and the following chapter to properly introduce you to how these two disciplines relate and interrelate.

In this chapter, we will introduce the basic financial framework by which real estate developers approach their work. Next, we will introduce some basic concepts and terminology that describes how real estate functions within a capitalist system. The following section will review the ways that banks and investors define, organize, and measure real estate (in comparison with other investment classes) and among the different types of real estate types, including alternative housing models. Finally, we will describe the components of a financial analysis of real estate and the basic forms of reporting those results. This framing will provide important foundational knowledge for you as more advanced analytical approaches are introduced in subsequent chapters (e.g. pro forma).

As we advocate for a people-centered real estate development model in this book, it is critical to explain what a profit-centered model looks like. Given that this profit-centered model is the predominant approach employed in practice, this and Chapter 4 will provide insights and a baseline for those seeking to depart from the norm and seek out more people-centered practices.

Real Estate as a Class of Investment

For much of human history, people have exchanged goods and services and used some form of money (Passari and Rey 2015). But the modern notion of the economy, a global, linked, and networked system of monetary flows impacting our overall wealth and well-being is relatively new. Karabell (2014) writes that it really was not until the Great Depression of the 1930s that people broadly appreciated and understood how much people are tied to one another through our financial relationships. Today's understanding of the economy helps frame how to think about real estate. It is one of many classes of investments for the capital that travels across the planet, seeking growth.

Wherever there is money, whether it belongs to a pension fund for teachers in California or an heiress in Monaco, that money wants to grow. More precisely, the people who own that money want it to grow. For the teachers, they want their pension fund to grow so that it can deliver interest in the form of pension checks for retirees. For the heiress, she wants her wealth to grow so she can live off of interest from investments and keep the principal funds intact – to be able to leave such an inheritance to her own children. For both the pensioners and the heiress, the key challenge is to find a home (or homes) for their money so that it will grow. Such money can be invested in securities or bonds, in private equity accounts or commodities, or it can be invested in real estate (See Figure 3.1).

Figure 3.1   Renovated harbor walk in the Seaport District adjacent to the North End in Boston, MA, 2019. The real estate in the seaport district has received considerable investment through the early twenty-first century. By Edward Orde, CC BY-SA 4.0. https://creativecommons.org/licenses/by-sa/4.0, via Wikimedia Commons.

Depending on any single investor's needs, goals, and tolerance for risk, the choice of which class of investment they make will vary. The broader economic system that we all live in governs that choice. Our very interconnectedness means that it might not be an absurd scenario to imagine that the heiress from Monaco might be best served by being a part owner in a football stadium in Cleveland. Likewise, a teacher's pension fund from California may find itself purchasing an office building in Puerto Rico. In just the same way that a salaried worker might have their 401(k) invested in a mix of stock and bonds, anyone with any wealth may see advantages to a mix of investments across classes including real estate.

This internationalization of investment has profound implications for real estate development and planning. The examples presented in the previous chapter around a North End property owner struggling with renovation decisions needs to be understood within the broader context of how the investment decisions of hundreds of millions of people globally can shift both supply and demand in the North End and everywhere else. A choice by a real estate developer to build a new hotel adjacent to the North End will drastically impact that small property owner's own renovation decisions, but the real estate developer is not acting independently. They are motivated by a need for profit, a need to generate returns to their investors, and a need for their "product" to be attractive as an investment in competition with securities, bonds, treasuries, commodities, and other real estate investments.

A neighborhood plan for the North End has to recognize and engage with this reality or such a plan will fail. That is why we see planning commissions, committees, and other agencies widely controlled by real estate and business interests. The Growth Machine theory suggests that the players in the real estate and development professions in every community have the most to gain from local planning decisions, so they play a disproportionate role in such local government institutions through volunteering (or very low wage work) (Logan and Molotch 2012). There are exceptions and Logan and Molotch have written persuasively about how important it is for local governments to escape this pattern and to elect independent citizens to such planning bodies, those without a financial interest in growth and development. But local government political campaigns cost money, lawn signs, door knocking, phone banks, mailings, and those with a monetary stake in how planning sets the ground rules for real estate development will pay those bills.[1]

Basic Real Estate Concepts

While the focus of this book is on real estate *development*, this chapter offers a short tutorial on the more general field of real estate. The buying and selling of property without the development, redevelopment dimensions.

A good place to begin with is a definition of real estate: "Property consisting of land and the buildings on it, along with its natural resources such as crops, minerals, or water" or the business itself "the profession of buying, selling, or renting land, buildings, or housing" (Oxford English Dictionary 2020).

Legal scholars like to say that real property is akin to a bundle of sticks: the right to occupy, right to build, right to mine, air rights, right to grant easements across. Each of these rights can be bought or sold. The ubiquitous single-family home is generally bought and sold with all of these rights, a fee simple sale (Figure 3.2). But not always, sometimes a single-family home could be part of a homeowner's association which might constrain those rights, including the right to lease, the terms of leases, the right to make improvements, to change the color of the home, or even to erect "for sale" signs. Condominiums have even fewer sticks in the bundle, an owner has only a vote (among all of the condominium units in an association) in deciding when to repair a roof or repave a parking lot. Condominiums are run through elected boards who make these kinds of decisions, including setting a monthly fee to cover collective costs like snow plowing or shared utilities (Figure 3.3).

Figure 3.2 1925 Single family home in Bryan, Texas, United States. Larry D. Moore, CC BY-SA 4.0. https://creativecommons.org/licenses/by-sa/4.0, via Wikimedia Commons.

Figure 3.3 Condominium home in New Alipore neighborhood of Kolkata, India. Courtesy of Uma Edulbehram.

Fortunately, the vast litany of bundles or rights any given property owner might possess are, by law, recorded with a deed in a local government, publicly accessible registry. These deeds are formal documents that convey ownership in real property from one entity to another and contain covenants (or amendments) that provide details on limitations or restrictions. As part of any property transfer, it is the responsibility of an investor to conduct due diligence through a title search to gain confidence of what precisely they are buying and whether it has any encumbrances attached.

The most common encumbrance that will come up in such a title search is a mortgage. A mortgage is simply the name for a real property loan and involves the purchaser putting a down payment toward the purchase and then conveying temporary interest in the subject property to the bank (for the term of the mortgage) as a guarantee in the case of default. If the purchaser fails to pay back the loan, the bank acquires title to the property – per the covenants recorded with the deed at the time of the purchase. This foreclosure is a lose-lose proposition, certainly for the borrower but also for the bank, which suddenly is faced with an array of legal costs to acquire clear title to a property that they have to protect and maintain until they can sell it. Banks prefer to just collect monthly payments from their borrowers, with all that interest (See Figure 3.4).

A key question around mortgages are the terms: how long, at what interest rate, and with what associated fees? Residential, owner-occupied homes can usually obtain 30-year loans, though shorter increments are available (more on this later in the chapter). Interest rates are usually tied to broader market trends and the Federal Reserve Bank's federal funds rate. For a given property, the rate will also be based on the type of property (owner-occupied or investment), the use (residential, commercial, or industrial), and the creditworthiness of the borrower. Over the last several decades, interest rates have fluctuated between 8% and 3% for borrowers with excellent credit, for owner-occupied residential properties, higher for others.

Land and building values derive from a myriad of factors, including location, condition, overall market conditions, and planning and development regulations (See Figures 3.5 and 3.6). These regulations, like zoning discussed earlier, can restrict property values in a downzoning example (like limiting the height of office towers) or increase values in an upzoning example (like allowing multifamily housing in a zone historically limited to just single-family housing). Values can be estimated with the aid of a professional appraiser. Appraisers look at value through three types of methodologies: (1) sales comparison approach, (2) income approach, and (3) cost approach. The sales comparison approach is how websites like Zillow and Trulia give estimates of home value, they compile data from relatively recent sales (generally 6–12 months) on comparable properties with regard to size, use, age, condition, density, and location. A professional appraiser

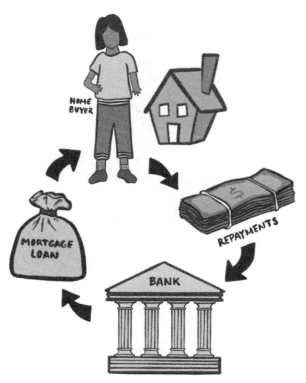

Figure 3.4 Homeowner's traditional mortgage model diagram. By Uma Edulbehram.

would take those comparables (comps) and adjust them up or down in value depending on how they might differ from the subject of their appraisal. If an appraiser was seeking to estimate the market value for a three-bedroom, 2,000 square-foot home on one acre of land, they would look for at least 3–5 recent sales in the same neighborhood. One might be a two-bedroom, 1,000 square feet on a half-acre sold at $200,000 and the other a six-bedroom, 4,000 square-foot home on two acres that sold at $800,000. If the two comps were similar to the subject property in all other ways, e.g., age, use, condition, location, then the small home's value would be doubled to arrive at $400,000. Likewise, the large home's value would be halved to also arrive at $400,000.

In the real world, the numbers never add up so neatly, and other adjustments are always needed. The finished attic adds some value to a comp, the dilapidated garage takes away value from another comp. Then there is the question of whether these recorded transactions the appraiser is using are arms-length transactions. Were they all fully and openly marketed or were they sold to a relative? Or was the

Figure 3.5 Row of Victorian houses exemplary of dense real estate in San Francisco, California. August 2016. Tobias Kleinlercher / Wikimedia Commons / Public domain.

Figure 3.6 Instance of sparsely populated real estate outside Oxford, Mississippi. Courtesy of Uma Edulbehram.

Figure 3.7 Storefront for sale in St. Louis, Missouri. March 2015. Paul Sableman from St. Louis, MO, CC BY 2.0. https://creativecommons.org/licenses/by/2.0, via Wikimedia Commons

seller under duress and they sold quickly without realizing market value? These are all questions that appraisers consider, issues not necessarily integrated into online (and free) property estimates.

The second appraisal strategy is the income approach. While the sales comparative approach is widely used in owner-occupied real estate, the income approach is reserved largely for income-generating real estate, like apartment, office, retail (Figure 3.7), and industrial buildings. An appraiser looks at how much profit a property generates by collecting data on costs and income over time. The difference between costs and income is the net operating income (NOI). Appraisers tend to include comparative income generating properties in the use of this approach, to essentially use information on these comps' NOI and their sales price to estimate the subject property's value.

The final appraisal method, the cost approach, is the least frequently used and simply estimates the cost of construction to arrive at an estimated market value. Rarely does the cost approach give a full picture of market price, but for new structures and as a compliment to the other two methods it can offer valuable information.

Buying and selling land and buildings happens to be a lucrative enterprise. During an upmarket, a property can be purchased on margin or with a loan and an investor can then make superficial improvements (or none at all) and then sell the property with a gain, repaying their debt. The 1949 Housing Act described in Chapter 1 regularized the mortgage industry and subsequent federal legislation introduced a secondary mortgage market that has meant that for decades capital for real estate has been very free flowing (Martinez 2000).

For such purchase and sale to be profitable, rising prices are the ideal environment for an investor, but not a requirement. A savvy investor can identify properties that have depressed prices relative to market values and then make improvements that enhance the price, all at a cost below expected profit at the time of sale. For example, if a 2,000 square-foot single-family home has a non-operating septic system it may sell for a reduced price of $100,000. If an investor puts down 20% on the purchase ($20,000) and borrows the balance from a bank with a 30 year mortgage at a 5% interest rate (with expected monthly payments of $630) they also have to contend with property taxes (in the range of $5,000 per year, though varies tremendously by locale), property insurance (will be required by lender and can be upwards of $1,000 per year), and other possible utility costs (public water, trash collection, and other municipal fees can approach another $1,000 per year).

Totaled up, the investor can expect that if they hold the property for one year and use that time to arrange to connect the home to a public sewer system (at a cost of approximately $25,000) then their total out of pocket costs for the year might be $39,560 ($7,560 for mortgage payments, $7,000 for property taxes, insurance, and utilities, and the $25,000 for the upgrade to sewer). The investment will be worthwhile if they can sell the property for not just $140,000 but enough to cover any real estate agent sales commission (as much as 5% or 6% of sales price), local or state government fees or taxes (varies widely by jurisdiction but can be in the 3% range), and profit from the investment (at least 5%-10%). If they were able to rent out the property during the duration of the sewer upgrade, that will help with profit, but lack of sanitary bathroom facilities makes that unlikely and a sewer upgrade could be expected to take an entire year.

This entire exercise was intended to demonstrate how real estate, at a most basic level works in the US. In order for any investor to take on this troubled sewer-less property, they would need to believe that they could make the sewer upgrade and sell the property for at least $165,000. An appraisal could help the investor understand if this target sales price a year later was realistic, as could a more informal review of what similar homes were selling for in the neighborhood.

We began this example by introducing the neighborhood as one with stable housing prices; a sudden downturn in prices could jeopardize this investment, as might a sudden rise in prices make the investment even more lucrative. The 2020 coronavirus pandemic taught us that sudden changes can come from nowhere and surprises should always be expected and planned for.

Real estate investment in places with appreciating prices allows us to explore a number of key concepts that will be important later in the book. Taking the example above, let us instead imagine a growing neighborhood with prices rising. Let us begin with where the above example left off, a new purchase of a $160,000 home, with sewer improvements. Instead of a defective home, now we turn to the case of a home in need of no major improvements. The complication we will introduce here is of an appreciating housing market, 3% increase in prices per year.

As with the previous example, we will make a 20% down payment (generally required by banks) on a 30-year mortgage at a 5% interest rate, that would be $32,000 down and with the help of amortization schedules we arrive at a monthly mortgage payment of $947 ($11,364 per year). This kind of investment can take many forms, it can be the investor's primary residence, it can be rented out, it can be subdivided or turned into condominiums, or it can be flipped. Each choice has its own risks and rewards. We will focus here on a very common investment: to rent out the house for a set number of years. The aim would be for an investor to recoup in rent the costs of their mortgage and all other expenses, ideally generating a small surplus to cover their own costs and a reserve for capital expenditures. In time, this investment is worthwhile as the original mortgage is paid down and the property appreciates in value.

Using some of the same expenses recorded above, an investor would need to consider annual property taxes ($5,000), property insurance ($1,000), and other utility costs (public water, sewer, trash collection, and other municipal fees for another $1,000) when they conducted a market analysis to assess what the rental rate might be. Given the many systems of a home and its expensive components: roof, foundation, HVAC (heating, ventilation, air conditioning, and cooling), electrical, plumbing, siding, landscaping, parking/garage, a savvy investor will anticipate capital expenditures during the life of their investment, which for simplicity we will estimate at $5,000 per year. Together, that means with the mortgage and all of these expenses, the investor's costs per year will be $23,364 or $1,947 per month. If the market supports rental payments in that range (say $2,000 per month), then the investor can likely cover their costs on an annual basis, while paying down the mortgage and benefiting from appreciation. Mortgages take a very long time to pay down, early payments are mostly interest, but after ten years that original $128,000 loan ($160,000 less the 20% down payment) could be cut down to $118,000 and a rising market at 3% annual appreciation could mean a sales price as high as $215,000. If the investor successfully kept their costs below their rental income and sold after ten years, they would expect to earn approximately $10,000 from equity they paid off in their mortgage and $55,000 from appreciation, less any sales commissions, taxes, or fees paid (roughly $17,000). With that initial down payment of $32,000 and not so insignificant effort, this real estate investor made a profit over ten years of $48,000 (or $4,800 per year, an annual return of 15%) (See Figure 3.8). Consider this another way, if the investor

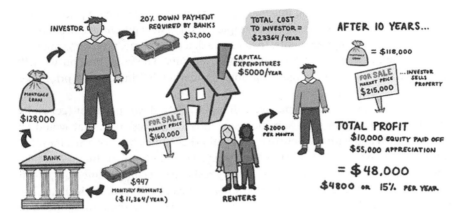

Figure 3.8 Diagram of ten year real estate investment. By Uma Edulbehram.

had put their money in a savings account, they might generate 2%, a certificate of deposit perhaps 3%, stocks or bonds might yield as high as 8%–10%.

It should now be no surprise that real estate investing is a big business. It attracts capital from anywhere and anyone looking for large returns and can tolerate risk. Homes do not always appreciate and $5,000 per year in capital improvements is not always enough. Renters don't always pay their rent and housing court (and lawyers) are very expensive.

These examples can be helpful in illustrating the types of expenses and returns that are possible in a simple case of purchasing a home. Real estate investing comprises so much more than this, including duplexes, apartments, mobile home communities, retail buildings, office buildings, industrial buildings, etc. For each class of real estate, a complex set of rules and norms exist in considering how to invest and how to gauge whether an investment will be fruitful.

In none of this analysis is the investor terribly concerned with the way that their purchase might impact people. Both the academic study and practice of real estate investment is quite individualistic and focused on how to achieve profit. There are some exceptions, like when the investor advertises for tenants. Each locality and state will have a slew of regulations on how an investor can advertise, screen, manage, and evict (if necessary) a tenant. The very use of the property is highly governed by local zoning and use requirements, such that a pizza shop might be OK but a hair salon might not. Federal and state tax laws can make property taxes deductible or count the depreciation of real property as credits on owed taxes. These kinds of public restrictions of our example investor suggest that the spreadsheet analysis, the close examination of costs, amortization schedules, return on investment, they all need to be executed in light of public policy and planning. Those tools and techniques of a real estate investor cannot be wielded in a vacuum, they are embedded in public goals for a given community.

Basic Financials Conclusion

The math is not complicated: if a real estate investment can generate sufficient income to cover all costs, while offering a return to the investor, then we have a healthy real estate market. When those numbers don't add up and an investor can not cover their costs, they will be highly motivated to reduce costs, to ensure a profitable investment – that is where problems start. Reducing costs means deferring maintenance and repairs. Eventually, such cost cutting can have a negative impact on the appearance of buildings and send a message to others looking to live, work, or invest in a neighborhood: stay away.

Planners can work closely with real estate investors, managers, and developers to prevent those problems from happening – through public subsidies, rezoning, and neighborhood and community planning, public policies can directly impact the mathematics of real estate investment and help keep markets healthy and functioning. Failed real estate markets, where buildings are poorly maintained or even abandoned, require massive public funds and eminent domain authority through redevelopment – something nobody wants.

While the financial lessons in this chapter have been simple, the next chapter introduces some more sophisticated tools to analyze the financials of a real estate development. These two chapters help bringing the perspectives of planners and developers together around a shared understanding of how investment decisions are made and what it takes to create people-centered real estate development that achieves public and community goals beyond pure profit for investors.

Note

1 It is worth noting here that planners themselves have been encouraging each other to run for elected office for generations, with the hope that they, as independent professionals disinterested in the flows of capital driving real estate development, are the best candidates for political office (Grooms and Frimpong Boamah 2018). While many such planners have won elected office and many have risen in the political ranks, without the financial backing of a wealthy coalition winning can be difficult.

Bibiography

Grooms, W. and Frimpong Boamah, E. (2018). Toward a political urban planning: learning from growth machine and advocacy planning to 'plannitize' urban politics. *Planning Theory* [online] 17 (2): 213–233. doi: 10.1177/1473095217690934.

Karabell, Z. (2014). *The Leading Indicators: A Short History of the Numbers That Rule Our World*. New York: Simon and Schuster.

Logan, J. and Molotch, H. (2012). *The City as a Growth Machine*, 2e. Routledge.

Martinez, S.C. (2000). The Housing Act of 1949: its place in the realization of the American dream of homeownership. *Housing Policy Debate* 11 (2): 467–487. doi: 10.1080/10511482.2000.9521374.

Passari, E. and Rey, H. (2015). Financial flows and the international monetary system. *The Economic Journal* [online] 125 (584): 675–698. doi: 10.1111/ecoj.12268.

4

Pro Forma and Financial Analysis

In the previous chapter, we explored a simple example of a house investment. Reviewing some of the numbers:

Purchase price of a $160,000, 2,000 square-foot home

An appreciating housing market, 3% increase in prices per year.

Investor makes a 20% down payment on a 30-year mortgage at a 5% interest rate ($32,000 down and with the help of amortization schedules we arrive at a monthly mortgage payment of $947 [$11,364 per year])

Income:

Rental income per month ($2,000)

Expenses:

Annual property taxes ($5,000)

Property insurance ($1,000)

Other utility costs (public water, sewer, trash collection, and other municipal fees, $1,000)

Capital investments for home systems (averages $5,000 per year).

In Chapter 3, we roughly sketched out these numbers, did some basic arithmetic, and concluded that the investment can be profitable. Now, we will turn to the real estate finance world and introduce more sophisticated nomenclature and accounting techniques to conduct the same analysis.

First, we need to be able to compare investing in this house project with any other possible investments, in securities, bonds, commodities, etc. We do this by

Buildings for People: Responsible Real Estate Development and Planning, First Edition.
Justin B. Hollander and Nicole E. Stephens.
© 2023 John Wiley & Sons, Inc. Published 2023 by John Wiley & Sons, Inc.

Figure 4.1 Instance of uneven real estate development in New York City. Investors likely calculated future value of the renovations of the right-hand side home to be financially profitable. Courtesy of Uma Edulbehram.

using **Present Value** to look at where we might end up with a real estate project and estimate how much money that would mean today (See Figure 4.1). The time value of money helps us understand if I had $100 today, it is always better than $100 at some point in the future because that money could have been invested and grown. If we are excited about a real estate investment being worth $1 million in the future, let's first discount that money and calculate what that $1 million is worth today before diving into a project.[1]

The formula for making this calculation is:

$$FV = PV(1 + i)^n$$

FV = future value

PV = present value

i = interest

n = term

Discounting is really just the opposite of compounding: when we have $1,000 today, if it is invested in a savings account at a 3% annual interest rate then the compounding will result in a Future Value of $1,344 after 10 years. In Microsoft Excel, the formula looks like this: [=1000*((1+0.03)^10)]. Likewise, when we have a future value in 10 years of $1 million and annually discounted at 3%, the Present Value is $744,094. To calculate discounting in Excel, the formula looks like this: [=1000000*(1/((1+0.03)^10))].

For our single-family home example (Figure 4.2), we want to know what the compounded interest rate will be for our project, to be able to compare it against other possible investments.

If we know Present Value ($160,000) and because home values are expected to rise 3% per year over the next ten years, we can estimate Future Value to be $215,026.

$$FV = (\$215,026) = PV(\$160,000)(1 + 0.3)^{10 \text{ years}}$$

Figure 4.2 Single Family Home in Falls Church, VA. By Ser Amantio di Nicolao – Own work, CC BY-SA 3.0. https://commons.wikimedia.org/w/index.php?curid=84393242.

We return now to a concept briefly introduced in the last chapter when discussing real estate appraisal: net operating income (NOI). NOI is used in financial analysis to calculate cash flow and, consequently, whether a proposed project will be profitable. To begin, we estimate potential gross income, that is the full rental income a property might generate, prior to any discounts or losses due to non-payment or other expenses. The gross income can be calculated by multiplying the rent per square feet by total square feet occupied. In the case of our single-family home example, the rent might be calculated at $1 per square foot,[2] per month or $2,000 per month for our 2,000 square-foot house ($24,000 per year).

Next, we estimate vacancy, missed rent payments, or other rent concessions that might occur. With a stable property, it is fair to use a 5–10% vacancy rate (Miles, Netherton, and Schmitz 2015 p. 208). Finally, we consider operating expenses like those enumerated in Chapter 2; however here we exclude debt service payments (mortgage payments) and capital costs. For this example, those operating expenses would include:

Annual property taxes ($5,000)

Property insurance ($1,000)

Other utility costs (public water, sewer, trash collection, and other municipal fees, $1,000)

Operating Expenses = $7,000

NOI then equals $24,000 (Potential Gross Income) minus $7,000 (Operating Expenses) = $17,000.

Next, we subtract Capital Expenditures (the irregular costs involved in painting, installing a new roof, repairing a broken toilet, etc.) and Financing costs (monthly mortgage payments) from NOI. Using figures from above:

Cash Flow = $17,000 [NOI] – $5,000 [Capital Expenditures] – $11,364 [Financing costs, mortgage payments]

Cash Flow = $636

Capitalization Rates (cap rates) provides a mechanism to estimate the value of a real estate development project. All you need is to know cash flow and NOI for a given property. Cap rates represent the relationship between NOI and the purchase price of a property (Miles et al. 2015). With the above example we see that with a purchase price of $160,000 and an NOI of $17,000, the Cap rate is the NOI divided by the purchase price – 10.6%. Unfortunately, this Cap rate only applies to a single year. A more precise way to run such an analysis is to consider multi-year costs through a discounted cash flow valuation.

By considering the present value of future revenues and potential sale of the property, we can better understand whether the project is a sensible investment (See Figure 4.3). The key variable needed to do so is to understand the investor's ***Required Rate of Return***, what can be thought of as the ***market "risk-free" rate of return*** – the current rate on a Treasury bond, which has no risk, and an estimated ***risk premium*** (Miles et al. 2015 p. 212). Then, using these same numbers, the investor calculates the terminal value, the value after a specified amount of time, say a ten-year term. Here, the formula is Terminal Value = NOI divided by Cap Rate: a projected higher NOI in ten years might be $22,000, divided by the same 10.6% NOI equals $207,500 (alternatively, you can use the Future Value calculated above based on market conditions of 3% annual appreciations, $215,026).

Figure 4.3 Recently completed real estate development project in Cambridge, Massachusetts. Courtesy of Uma Edulbehram.

A discount rate (as discussed earlier in the chapter) is then used to calculate Present Value of each year of cash flow, then subtracting development costs (see Table 4.1).

A couple limitations before proceeding: this analysis does not consider closing costs associated with purchasing and selling real property (real estate agent commission, title insurance, legal fees, recording fees), which were estimated to be $17,000 in Chapter 3. Nor does this pro forma consider taxes – including conveyance and income taxes at the local, state, and federal levels. These taxes or lack thereof, can be major drivers of an investment decision. Since taxes vary widely from state to state and can be impacted depending on the proposed use and whether certain historic or low-income tax credit might be available, we consider here a simplistic view of what this cash flow pro forma analysis tells us, omitting taxes and closing costs.

Because of cash flow from rent and increased property value, after ten years, we would expect that the project would yield $55,253 more than if we had simply invested our initial capital ($32,000 for down payment) in a 10% interest bearing savings account. As Brueggeman and Fisher (2022) explain in their seminal textbook on real estate finance, this $55,253 shows that an investor in this

Table 4.1 Simplified cash flow pro forma.

Year	Cash Flow	Present Value (10%) *
1	$636	$578
2	$668	$552
3	$701	$527
4	$736	$503
5	$773	$480
6	$812	$458
7	$852	$437
8	$895	$417
9	$940	$399
10	$215,026	$82,902
Total Present Value=		$87,253
Less Initial Investment=		$32,000
Net Present Value=		$55,253

*A 10% discount rate is included here, such that these cash flows could have instead been invested elsewhere; so this Present Value amount captures the time value of money.

single-family home project could hope to earn more than a 10% Internal Rate of Return on the investment, or they can earn that 10% return and put an extra $55,253 into the down payment, reducing their mortgage and hence their monthly payments – which also would enhance monthly cash flow.

The option of reducing debt on a mortgage might sound attractive, but generally frowned upon in finance circles (Miles, Netheron, Schmitz 2015 p. 220). Businesses are always trying to leverage their assets as much as possible in order to facilitate growth. The more they borrow, the more opportunities they have for big returns on their investments. Of course, the more debt, the riskier a project for other investors besides the real estate developer. Those other investors (like banks) will charge higher interest rates on loans which have a lower loan-to-value ratio (e.g. a smaller relative down payment). Likewise, highly leveraged projects will require equity investors to demand higher shares of ownership, in exchange for this higher risk.

With these basic calculations, we might conclude that the single-family home investment is a good one. Not so fast. We have made numerous assumptions here; it is critical to interrogate how sensitive our conclusions are to small changes in these assumptions. Through a sensitivity analysis, we re-run the pro forma by making dozens of adjustments to those assumptions to see how robust the project's projected profitability really is (Figure 4.4).

A sensitivity analysis means starting with the basic assumptions around market conditions; how confident are we in the 3% expected growth rate in property values? What would happen to our pro forma if the terminal value of the house was much lower and growth rates were closer to 2%? What about NOI and Capital Expenditures? If we modify our assumptions for these and consider a worst-case scenario; a 20% vacancy rate (on average) or that the house needs significantly more capital improvements, driving up the annual capital expenditures to $7,500 per year. Together these could drive down our annual cash flow, threatening the viability of the project.

Given the outsized role that borrowed money plays in real estate development, it is important here to review a couple key concepts. In Miles et al. (2015) the authors argue that two metrics largely govern whether lenders will make a loan: Debt Service-Coverage Ratio and Loan-to-Value Ratio. These are not overly complex ideas, simple arithmetic really.

Loan-to-Value Ratio is the loan amount divided by the property value. For our example in this chapter, that would be: $128,000 [property mortgage]/$160,000 [purchase price] = 80%. Not a big surprise, we began this project knowing we were going to invest 20% as a down payment, leaving a balance of 80%. We started there because lenders do not like LTVs much higher than 80% and in many circumstances will require it to be even lower.

Debt Service-Coverage Ratio (DSCR) is calculated by taking the NOI and dividing it by the Annual Debt Service (those annual mortgage payments). For our project,

Figure 4.4 Instance of duplex home renovations in Cambridge, Massachusetts (left-hand side) contrasted with unrenovated duplex (right-hand side). Demonstrates uneven development practices based on mathematical modeling. Courtesy of Uma Edulbehram.

that means $17,000 [NOI]/$11,364 [annual debt service] = 1.49. This ratio helps capture, for the lender, the general buffer between monies being brought in from income sources (e.g. rent) and the loan payments that the developer is going to have to make. The higher the ratio, the less risky the loan is for the lender. Lenders prefer that this DSCR is between 1.20 and 1.60 (Miles et al. 2015; Mathew et al. 2021).

Lenders will use these two metrics together to assess the strengths and weaknesses of a proposed project as part of their decision as to whether to issue a loan and what the terms of that loan will be. They will also consider many other relevant factors, like the composition of the development team, prior experience, market conditions, local government approval likeliness, and creditworthiness of future tenants. If lenders are not happy with any of these dimensions of a proposed project, they will not move forward with a loan or impose burdens that make the calculations for a developer's profits less tenable.

* * *

While we started this chapter by looking at the example of a single-family home, the mathematics introduced here can also be applied to commercial or industrial properties, to investments of any size and scale. The bigger and more complicated a project, the more complicated the financial analysis will need to be, considering those closing costs, taxes, and a range of ever more complex debt structuring to favor the best possible internal rate of return. The ten-year window introduced here likewise can be adjusted in a more sophisticated pro forma that tells the investor what the ideal holding time for a property might be. Of course, market conditions will determine when selling a property makes the most sense, but before starting any investment the tools introduced in this chapter can allow for a better understanding of the range of possible futures and guide the army of under-writers, lenders, appraisers, lawyers, accountants, and urban planners who are involved in any real estate development.

There are numerous assumptions built into the formulas introduced here. First, they all presume that financial interests are paramount in a real estate development project. Could not an internal rate of return on "well-being" or "happiness" be equally justifiable? When projecting into the future, are 3–4% annual growth rates even sustainable in an environmental sense – what might be the implications for whole human-ecological systems which are continuing to grow and expand? The units of analysis in these pro formas are limited to the site, the investors, and the global financial markets, with little input from neighbors or surrounding communities. Annual positive cash flows might look good on a spreadsheet, but what if they come at the expense of struggling tenants and lead to eviction. Widespread evictions can overwhelm social services in a place and directly spur homelessness. None of these considerations enter into the pro forma, it is simply a tool to assess financial performance.

The lessons in this and the previous chapter helps present what makes an investment worthwhile, but Chapters 1 and 2 introduced a model of what true people-centered development looks like: making affordable housing a primary concern, while also focusing on community amenities, access to public transportation, and outdoor public spaces at the secondary level. We argue here that the financial imperatives of profit cannot be ignored, but their proper place remains at that tertiary level.

As we turn in the next five chapters to the stages of real estate development and the many actors involved in a project, the macro challenges of making people-centered development happen will come to the fore. Developers do not ignore these broader concerns; instead, the interplay between the narrow financial performance of a development and its community impacts is the exact place where planning comes in. A solid planning process provides a balance between the investment needs of a project and neighborhood needs and issues, ideally shaping a hierarchy like we introduced in Figure 2.17 "Components of People-centered Development".

An effective planning process can structure a real estate development and planning project by starting at the site selection stage, covered in the next chapter, and moving all the way through construction, covered in Chapter 9. Planners and developers are in an intricate dance to ensure that the people who live, work, and play in a place can enjoy the benefits of new development – while not ignoring the role that profit inevitable will play. If the pro forma analysis does not add up, if a project is not profitable, then it will not happen. The remaining chapters provide a roadmap for how planners and developers can work together to ensure that real estate development projects do more than improve the bottom line, that they enhance communities for people.

Notes

1 A related consideration here is inflation. When inflations rates are high, the purchasing power of money diminishes, so investment gains might be sought to preserve the original asset's value – just enough growth to beat out the loss that inflation impacts.
2 $1/square foot is a completed contrived figure, purely for illustration purposes. Price-per-foot rental rates will vary drastically from neighborhood to neighborhood, region to region.

Bibliography

Brueggeman, William B., and Jeffrey Fisher. (2022). *Real Estate Finances and Investments*, 11th edition. New York: McGraw-Hill Education.

Grooms, W. and Frimpong Boamah, E. (2018). Toward a political urban planning: learning from growth machine and advocacy planning to 'Plannitize' urban politics. *Planning Theory* [online] 17 (2): 213–233. doi: 10.1177/1473095217690934.

Mathew, P., Issler, P., and Wallace, N. (2021). Should commercial mortgage lenders care about energy efficiency? Lessons from a pilot study. *Energy Policy* 150: 112137. doi: 10.1016/j.enpol.2021.112137.

Miles, Mike E., Laurence M. Netherton, and Adrienne Schmitz. (2015). Real Estate Development–5th Edition: Principles and Process. Washington, DC: Urban Land Institute.

real estate, n (2020). In: *OED Online*. [online] Oxford University Press. https://www-oed-com.ezproxy.library.tufts.edu/view/Entry/238664 (accessed July 2, 2022).

5

Site Selection

Before any real estate development can happen, a site for such development must first be identified. This chapter offers an introduction to the process a developer goes through to identify a site, the typical considerations they may make in their choice, and the need to satisfy community interests along the way. We conclude the chapter by highlighting the first of five case studies in the book. In the Mosaic on the Riverway case, the site selection process entailed more than tacit engagement with future neighbors; instead it involved a deeper and more sustained engagement. This kind of people-based development processes can put the residents and future users of a site at the center of site selection consideration by participating in community-engagement in an in-depth and deliberative manner where disempowered voices can be heard.

The development of real estate can mean major renovation of existing structures (Figure 5.1), substantial additions, or the acquisition of undeveloped land for new construction (Figure 5.2). Here we are excluding the kind of routine maintenance and capital improvements needed to regularly care for any building. Real estate development is about investing substantial funds in the expectation of attractive returns, it is not about just replacing a roof or repairing a parking lot.

The very spatial nature of development also means that latitude and longitude matter, the location where such investment occurs is, in many cases, the most important variable in determining an investment's profitability. In some circumstances a real estate developer may begin a project with their own inventory of land or buildings, seeking to construct a new house or put a major addition on a shopping center. For all other cases, developers spend their time scouring maps, market data, and for-sale listings to determine where they might build or renovate. What are they looking for? What kind of analysis do they undertake in their search? How do they compare options? What kind of due diligence is

Buildings for People: Responsible Real Estate Development and Planning, First Edition.
Justin B. Hollander and Nicole E. Stephens.
© 2023 John Wiley & Sons, Inc. Published 2023 by John Wiley & Sons, Inc.

Figure 5.1 Old courtyard house converted into cafe in Berlin, Germany. Courtesy of Uma Edulbehram.

Figure 5.2 Undeveloped urban plot in Philadelphia, Pennsylvania. Mike Linksvayer / Flickr / Public Domain.

required when making such comparisons? And, lastly, how does their decision intersect with the needs, desires, and rules imposed by the neighborhood and community where their site is located? These are the questions we will explore in this chapter.

The Hunt

The manner in which a developer begins to search for sites will be impacted by many factors, including the scale of their intended development (in terms of dollars and size), geographical constraints possibly due to state and local regulations (for example, public bodies vary drastically with regard to how welcoming they are to developers), and whether they have a tenant already in place for which they are developing and that tenant's requirements. With a tenant already lined up, that tenant's requirements may be the only driver in a developer's site selection process.

With whatever criteria they have in mind, a developer may hire a real estate agent or broker to assist them in finding sites and also assist in any negotiations that may result. That agent will ideally be an expert on their local geography and assist in understanding the history and prior use of properties of interest. This "hunt" for a site tends to be slow and can take anywhere from a couple months to a couple years.

If successful, the agent will bring several candidate properties to the attention of the developer, along with as much local and regional market data possible and information on the subject properties themselves. For each site, the developer should run pro forma analyses (see Chapter 4) to be able to weigh site acquisition costs (purchase price, fees, costs of any improvements, financing) against expected revenues.

In the example of a developer seeking to build a gas station for a corporate client, the ideal location might be along a busy road in a heavily populated part of town. If one site was a wooded, unimproved lot and the other was previously developed as a dry cleaner (Figure 5.3), the potential for environmental contaminants at the dry cleaner might make the unimproved lot more attractive. But if the dry cleaner was in a busier part of town and could generate greater traffic for the gas station, that extra risk might be worthwhile. It is that ability to make direct cost and revenue comparisons between locations that is at the core of the conventional site selection process.

The specific challenges of locations like dry cleaners are the unknowns related to environmental contamination. These properties, known as brownfields, are a common feature of the urban landscape – every former industrial location, gas station, trash transfer station, and dry cleaner could probably be classified as a

Figure 5.3 Potential development lot at former dry cleaner.

brownfield. The US Environmental Protection Agency (2018) defines a property whose expansion, redevelopment, or reuse may be complicated by the presence or potential presence of a hazardous substance, pollutant, or contaminant as a brownfield. Since they are common, the US EPA, US states, and countries across the planet have developed programs and incentives to reduce the complications associated with these properties.

The comparison a developer makes between a brownfield and an undeveloped site axiomatically called a greenfield needs to consider not only these public programs to reduce the risks and costs of brownfields (though low-interest loans, grants, and technical assistance) but also the broader public purpose of these programs. The brownfields movement was born in the late 1990s in response to concerns around the ill effects of urban sprawl (Hollander 2009). As we touched on in Chapter 1, building in undeveloped forests, on farms, and in sensitive environmental zones like bogs and wetlands, has many negative impacts on communities, and urban planners today generally recommend new building happen mostly in previously developed areas (Kunstler 1994; Frumkin 2002; Beauregard 2006). Few governments in North America have taken this recommendation too seriously (See Figures 5.4 and 5.5), but in Europe and parts of Asia, such anti-sprawl planning is dogma (Yang et al. 2008, Yuen 2011; Wu and Gaubatz 2013). With little in the way of enforcement, these smart growth programs focus primarily on funding and support to tip the scales for developers in making siting decisions toward previously built-up areas. Documented patterns of continued sprawling growth in the United States since the 1990s

Figure 5.4 Aftermath of Hurricane Harvey in Houston, Texas, indicative of the consequences of development over wetland habitat. U.S. Department of Defense / Larry E. Reid Jr.

Figure 5.5 Close-up view of the aftermath of Hurricane Harvey. Air Force Magazine / Flickr / Public Domain.

suggests that those government programs have done little to change the behavior of enough developers (Frumkin 2002; Lee 2020). Instead, these smart growth and brownfield initiatives have represented important incentives in just a limited number of cases (Hollander et al. 2010). The US EPA (2019) estimated that the number of brownfields in the United States was roughly 450,000. While the US EPA boasts about their successes on their website, hundreds of millions have been spent to convert only thousands of such brownfields, leaving most untouched (US EPA 2019).

While we might teach our urban planning students the importance of encouraging developers to choose a previously developed site over a greenfield, and various programs are out there to back up that encouragement, none of that fundamentally changes the pro forma analysis. If the former dry cleaner location (from the example earlier) is a less profitable site than the wooded lot, the developer will not (unless legally compelled to) choose that site. Which is a good segue to a review of what local and state governments do to legally compel such site selection choices.

The Role of Local Land Use Regulation

The codification of rules and regulations for land development were increasingly widespread in the United States by the middle of the twentieth century, as discussed in Chapter 1. Before that, local officials had ultimate discretion as to what could and could not be built. Today, such discretion is very limited in the United States and it is the written rules, maps, and regulations that are supposed to guide most real estate development. At least that is how we expect it to happen.

The practical application of those rules generally means that real estate developers can build, but they may not be able to build what they want to. The rules in a given municipality might allow for the construction of four single family homes on a two-acre parcel of land. The allowable use of land is known as by-right use. That is, an owner of the property can build or improve their land without any special approvals, only subject to building code compliance. Just about every non-government owned acre in America is zoned with some by-right use, single-family housing is the most common (Hirt 2015). A typical local government in New England zones more than 80% of their land area for single-family by-right use (Bronin 2021, Boston Fair Housing). Other zoning categories, for example higher density housing, retail, office, or industrial, can be sought by a property owner through a special permit process. These special permit hearings introduce additional discretion by local officials to weigh broader public needs.

After conducting their pro forma analysis, a developer may realize that current conditions make the four-house project (See Figure 5.6) unfeasible financially. Maybe banks are demanding too high interest rates on loans or local builders are asking for exorbitant wages or simply, real estate prices are falling and the

Figure 5.6 Single family plot flipped to four-house project in Cambridge, Massachusetts. Courtesy of Uma Edulbehram.

expected sales prices won't cover costs. Whatever the reason, the developer would approach local officials to explore alternative development scenarios for the two-acre parcel, perhaps building four duplex homes or just a single large apartment building. Here, those officials have much discretion.

Research has shown that local officials wield extensive discretion in such negotiations, providing various levels of relief to a developer to make their project profitable in exchange from everything from direct payments to cover infrastructure costs (like sewer extensions or roads), local amenities (like parks or schools), or even illegal payments in the form of bribes (Wallace 2004; Hirt 2015). In most parts of the US, these linkage or impact fees are informal, but in some places like Florida they are written into law.

Especially large or complex real estate development projects are always subject to this kind of negotiation. While the attention of much of the book to this point has been from the perspective of the real estate developer, here it is useful to reflect a bit on why local officials might want new development, whether it is the four houses on the two acres described above or a large, complex project like a multi-story office building or manufacturing facility. In such negotiations, what does the local government want?

The most compelling framework for considering this question is the Growth Machine, an idea briefly introduced in Chapter 2. Local officials are a broad category; they are comprised of elected officials, appointed officials, and professional staff. The elected officials are those residents who run for office, build coalitions, and raise money to do all of that. Appointed officials are generally part of elected officials' coalitions, supporters, or even donors to those election campaigns. Professional staff are civil servants, for the most part, and tend be apolitical. The Growth Machine theory tells us that both elected and appointed officials disproportionately make their living in industries related to construction and growth, professional staff usually do not have a financial stake in growth – except to the extent that they seek to be in the good graces of their employers, who do have that financial stake. There are also many local governments that depend on new real estate development fees to fund their very functions, thus paying the salaries of those professional staff (Hollander 2011).

When a real estate development happens in a community, those elected or politically appointed officials stand to benefit financially. The Planning Board Chair might own a lumber business that the developer purchases from to build houses. The Vice Chair of the Select Board may run a paving business that the developer, without breaking any laws, just might select for paving their new roads.

Beyond personal profit and wealth accumulation, local officials also see benefit in development through the fiscal impact of new growth. While we explored the costs of sprawl and the big picture range of negative fiscal impacts of low-density development in new greenfield location earlier in this chapter, the short-term fiscal impacts of new development can be quite positive. The immediate collection of new fees and property taxes from a real estate development project can mean a valuable infusion of cash into local accounts. Local officials sometimes seek "empire building" by attracting new sources of revenues to build new programs and initiatives (Figure 5.7). For political officials, like elected and appointed ones, this expansion of their responsibilities help get them re-elected or run for higher office. For examples, if a Mayor can successfully negotiate the construction of a new hospital and taxes generated from the project can be funneled into a new city-wide nutrition program, the Mayor's political capital has now risen.

Another dimension of new development is the indirect economic benefit for a community. The construction of just a single, 2,000 square foot detached home on a ½ acre of land might cost $150,000 in labor and materials. That is money that will largely go into the local economy through local purchases and the hiring of carpenters, plumbers, electricians, and others. The economic benefits of the development are reflected in the multiplier effect, a quantitative analysis of the jobs and revenue indirectly created. Local companies who hire specialized workers tend to have strong local multiplier effects, ranging from 1.5–2.0 (Domanski and Krzysztof 2010). If $150,000 is spent, a multiplier of 1.5 would indicate a total of $225,000 being put into the local community a result of the project.

Figure 5.7 Aerial view of San Jose, California, an area that has seen the explosive growth of the tech industry and Silicone Valley, 2014. Coolcaesar / Wikimedia Commons / CC BY-SA 3.0.

If we can expect those benefits for just a single home, what about that hospital project we mentioned earlier, which could cost $20 million to build and then another $10 million per year to operate – with hundreds of full-time jobs. For a large real estate development like a hospital, the economic impact is so profound it can be expected to alter the underlying economy in the community. Domanski and Krzysztof (2010) found that "the healthcare system in Carson City, Nevada, has created 0.49 additional jobs for every new healthcare job (multiplier = 1.49) as well as 35 cents of additional revenue for every dollar of new revenue in the healthcare sector (multiplier = 1.35)." Local officials can expect either a single giant project or the cumulative impact of many smaller projects to enhance the attractiveness of their community to such an extent that overall property values may increase. For a politician, that can be a very attractive outcome, enhancing the wealth of their property-owning constituents.

Unfortunately, the promises of economic benefits and (all too often) lies of boosters do not always come to fruition. The building of a new hospital might devastate an old hospital in the city. If the old hospital has to lay off employees and eventually shutter, the overall employment impact might be erased. The entire economic development enterprise is built on the notion that new development can help a community rise and bring in new employment, however research has been mixed on how much these new jobs help. The classic case is of the new Walmart built on the outskirts of town, bringing in hundreds of new jobs, but ultimately shutting down the small scale locally owned business in downtown. Stone (1997) preformed a matched case-control study, analyzing the long-term impacts on various sectors within retail across towns with and without Walmarts. Small towns with a Walmart particularly struggled, with home-furnishing, building material, and apparel sales.

Between personal profit, political opportunism, and the broader economic benefit new development might bring, it is rare in America for local officials to reject new real estate development. There are cases where officials have pushed back, but those tend to be due to concerns raised by impacted residents. In this next section, we introduce the many configurations of community involvement in real estate development and planning.

Community Engagement

In the US, the role of residents in directly shaping real estate development projects in their communities was fairly limited until the 1960s. That began to change with the growth of a range of environmental, civil rights, feminist, and other progressive movements that challenged just about all centers of power in society. Up until then, local officials would attempt to represent the interests of people who lived in impacted neighborhoods and if they failed, then those people would vote them out. Such electoral governance of real estate development gave rise to notable critics like Jane Jacobs and Sherry Artnstein. Jacobs (b. 1916) was a writer living in Greenwich Village, New York City (Figure 5.8), during a period of massive redevelopment through the city – led largely by the infamous master planner Robert Moses (Figure 5.9) (Caro 1975). Jacobs called for the reigning in of the planners, including Moses, demanding more review and approval of real estate and infrastructure projects at the neighborhood level. Likewise, Sherry Arnstein was worried about the role public hearings that were being held in cities across the country through her experience at the US Department of Housing and Urban Development and then working as a planning consultant. Her 1969 seminal journal article "A Ladder of Citizen Participation" argued that much of what local governments did regarding participatory processes were tokenism at best. She introduced a framework for planning to rise to higher levels in her metaphoric ladder, eventually reaching to partnership, delegated power, or even citizen control.

Due to the influence of Jacobs and Arnstein, community participation grew drastically in the 1970s and today most states and local governments have codified a real and meaningful role for public outreach and involvement in local development decision-making. That hardly means that community wishes and desires are regularly addressed, but at least the infrastructure exists for an airing of those grievances. Even the federal government joined this wave of

Figure 5.8 Activist Jane Jacobs at committee meeting in Greenwich Village in 1961. Phil Stanziola Kleinlercher / Wikimedia Commons / Public domain.

Figure 5.9 Planner Robert Moses with model for proposed Battery Bridge. C.M. Stieglitz / Wikimedia Commons / Public domain.

community involvement with the passage of the National Environmental Policy Act of 1970 (NEPA), which mandated that all federal actions be reviewed for environmental impacts and, if certain thresholds are met, requiring a community process for vetting impacts. Most states have likewise followed, which has meant that large real estate development projects almost always trigger either state or federal NEPA review.

NEPA and state-level equivalents require a thoughtful and thorough examination of how a project may contribute on its own or through cumulative impacts to environmental problems. The required scoping sessions with the general public provide an opportunity for people to voice their concerns about a project, whether those concerns are of an explicitly environmental nature or otherwise. NEPA then requires the developer to address each concern and explain their planned changes to the project, if any. These public processes rarely result in meaningful adjustments to projects, but they can. More importantly, they can drastically delay a project, costing the developer money and jeopardizing their pro forma analysis. Savvy project protesters know this and are effective at wielding these environmental reviews to nudge a developer towards their desired outcomes.

Local government reviews, like Design Review or Public Engagement Initiatives (Gordon 2016), can likewise introduce onerous public processes and meetings and can also be utilized by project opponents to stall a project and try to gain leverage over a developer. Many cities have developed their own NEPA equivalents but tend to focus on urban design or transportation dimensions. For example, Philadelphia's Comprehensive Plan for 2035 – which focuses on transportation, the environment, and community facilities (Citywide Vision Summary).

Another technique used in major real estate development projects is the Community Benefits Agreement (CBA). First used in limited cases in the early 2000s, the tool has gotten more widespread use in recent years as a mutually agreed upon contract between the real estate developer and the main opponents of a project (Salkin and Lavine 2008; Knapp and Hollander 2012). These opponents need to be well organized and legally registered as an entity in order to be a signatory to any binding agreement with the developer. This CBA is usually executed outside the formal local government approval process and seeks to ameliorate concerns emanating from the community around a new project. A developer in the LA Live Sports and Entertainment district negotiated one of the first major CBAs, leading to affordable housing, local hiring, and living wages (Saito and Truong 2014). The developer agrees to meet the conditions from their adversaries in exchange for the full support of those entities when the project officially goes before local government review. Like the linkages discussed earlier, these benefits accrue to a more focused group that are identified by the negotiating entity.

Some critics worry that because these CBAs are not negotiated by elected officials who are bound to represent their constituents that the public is not well served by them (Gross 2007).

The Public Meeting Itself

Public meetings are generally quite ineffective at generating any real engagement. Often, such a presentation will go beyond the analog poster board and handouts and include a Microsoft Powerpoint presentation. Maybe even the officials (or their consultants) will solicit input in real time through a Kahoot! Quiz or Poll Everywhere survey, asking members of the public to pull out their phones to interact digitally.

Outside of those stale public meetings, urban planners and designers today have embraced a wide range of other digital and analog tools for engaging people and soliciting input. This kind of Digital Community Engagement has been a leading edge for urbanists, where experimentation has led to innovation and excitement about what is possible. Particularly notable examples include Gordon, Schirra, and Hollander (2011), Evans-Cowley and Hollander (2010), and Hollander (2021).

Unfortunately, away from these award-winning experiments the norm remains that staid conference room and a largely analog interaction. Why might that be? We argue that much of the research, scholarship, and activism around Digital Community Engagement is misplaced. Despite the exciting stories on this kind of innovation that might grace the cover of *Planning Magazine* or be featured in a Slate blog entry, the quotidian business of government public engagement has rejected these approaches wholesale. That means it is time to rethink the role that online and digital processes can realistically take on. The good news is that alternative options actually exist that take full advantage of the potency and availability of the digital realm for improving the built environment.

Reversing the Directionality: The Role of Unobtrusive Data in Community Engagement

Consider Washington Square Park, it's 2020 (see Figure 5.10). The Park's famous marble triumphal arches soaring above the throngs of people. For this hypothetical case, imagine an anonymous donor wants to build a koi pond in the park's northwest corner (see Figure 5.11). This donor is anonymous to the public, but well known to the Mayor and leading politicians. The pond will be built, but the New York City Department of Parks and Recreation is obligated (by law) to run some form of consultative process with park user, including public meetings, prior to construction. Under today's typical frameworks, city

Figure 5.10 Washington Square Park in New York City. Jean-Christophe BENOIST, CC BY 3.0, via Wikimedia Commons.

Figure 5.11 Koi Pond in Seattle, Washington. brewbooks / Wikimedia Commons / CC BY-SA 2.0.

planners might enlist consultants with sketching out several versions of the koi pond design, maybe posting them on a special website, then holding a public meeting where members of the public may be able to voice their opinion on three different designs or even vote on their favorite. They might even hire outreach workers to hang around the park at different times to show people the koi pond designs and solicit feedback.

From our experience, this process is unlikely to be useful to the koi pond planners. Among the millions of annual visitors to the park, the City would be lucky with a few thousand comments total. Maybe a couple hundred people might come to one of the public meetings. The first question in evaluating public participation is whose opinions is the City hearing. Without representative participation, the feedback the city is hearing is biased, perhaps by age, race, ethnicity, religion, gender, income, or disability. The City might get information from people about the designs, but is it valid information? What do ordinary people know about the different designs for ponds? If they offer an opinion, how useful is it really? What people really might know is that the spot where they want to build it is where they like to picnic. But the public process might not accommodate that kind of feedback (the City has already decided they are going to build the pond and where, the band of openness to feedback is very narrow). Too often, these kinds of participation processes are closed in just such a way and are asking for feedback in ways that does not comport with people's actual ability to offer constructive input.

Now, imagine these city planners considered the question we posed above before starting this outreach: "how can people's knowledge and lived experience in a place contribute to shaping the built environment where they may live, work, or play?" With an estimated 12 million visitors per year, Washington Square Park is chock-full of knowledge and experience. In 1960, capturing any meaningful fraction of that knowledge and experience would have been impossible, but today, it's quite easy. We all leave behind a bevy of digital crumbs when we go places, when we surf online, and when we communicate with friends and family. We tell the world what we are worried about (Google searches), what sports teams we are following (social media), our hobbies (social media), our well-being and happiness (social media), where we travel to and how (mobile phones). In 2016, along with several colleagues, we developed the concept of "urban social listening" (Hollander et al. 2016). Unobtrusive, as opposed to the community engagement strategies described above, the notion is to understand what people know and how they live their lives based on those digital crumbs and use those insights to shape the built environment.

Urban Social Listening

As an emerging field, the systematic collection and analysis of microblog data and other digital crumbs as a means of understanding social issues has both strengths and weaknesses. It is a relatively fast and low-cost method of collecting freely volunteered opinions in real time from a wide range of the public on a wide range of topics. This is much simpler, cheaper, and faster than conducting surveys or interviews, for example. However, there are also limitations to consider. Use of social media to express opinions and sentiment is much more pervasive among certain age groups and among those who have more access to smartphones and computers than it is among other groups. Scholars have found that 88% of those ages 18–29 years reported using a social networking site of some kind, and of these 40% reported using Twitter (Gough et al. 2017; Sinnenberg et al. 2017) (see Figure 7). Twitter users are not representative of the US population, though use is higher among those under age 50 years and those living in urban rather than rural areas (Pew Research Center 2015). Demographically, users on Twitter also tend to be more educated and have higher incomes than the typical American (Wojak and Hughes 2019). Nationally, 30% of adult Americans comprise the lowest income group that the Pew Center studied (those with incomes under $30,000 per year), whereas 23% of Twitter users belonged to that income group. Among the next highest income group ($30,000–$74,999 per year), 33% of adult Americans fall into that group, where 36% of Twitter users earn that income range. The highest income group (over $75,000) saw the biggest gap between Twitter users (41%) and the general adult public (32%). Along gender and racial dimensions, Twitter users are quite representative of the general population. (ibid).

There are socioeconomic, linguistic, and cultural factors that may also impact use of social media. Thus, any social media or microblog data collected in this way cannot be said to be a random sample of the population to be studied, and it is important to be aware that key demographic groups may be underrepresented.

Uses of Sentiment Analysis

Sentiment analysis is a quasi-qualitative analytical method, a form of content analysis that can be applied to large data sets including social media data sets. Unlike traditional content analysis, in which a researcher reads through a document and codes certain words and phrases, sentiment analysis is a more automated process, using a sentiment dictionary and a computer program to analyze large data sets.

Sentiment analysis of microblogging data has been used to consider social issues in a variety of studies. For example, sentiment analysis can be used to assess the public mood in response to events. Bollen, Mao, and Pepe (2011) conducted a Twitter sentiment analysis in which they considered nationwide sentiment over a six-month period in 2008. They calculated a daily mood for their entire pool of data and correlated that with external events such as elections and holidays. Several other studies have compared microblogging sentiment analysis with the results of elections (O'Connor, Balasubramanyan, Routledge, and Smith 2010;

Gordon 2013), of special interest are those studies in which sentiment analysis has been used to compare different geographic areas. For example, Quercia et al. (2012) compared sentiment analysis of Tweets geotagged to different areas of London and found a strong correlation between expressed positive sentiment and higher socioeconomic variables for each area. A number of other studies have also used geotagged tweets to look at differences between different geographic areas (Lovelace et al. 2014; Mearns et al. 2014; Mitchell et al. 2013; Balduini et al. 2013; Bertrand, Bialik, Virdee, Gros, and Bar-Yam 2013; Antonelli et al. 2014).

Urban Planning and Design Applications of Microblog Sentiment Analysis

While the field is still new, Twitter sentiment analysis has been applied successfully to urban design and urban planning topics. Antonelli et al. and Balduini et al. (2013) look at Twitter as a way to assess reactions to city-scale events, while MacEachren et al. (2011) apply similar methods to crisis management. Lovelace et al. (2014) consider a very small scale, comparing how many visitors frequent different museums in Yorkshire, England, based on Tweets about the museums or Tweets sent from the geographic locations of the museums. Geotagged tweets have also been used to track movement of people over time (Fujisaka et al. 2010), to determine land use in urban environments, and to map the location of self-identified hipsters, bankers, and artists (Poorthuis and Zook 2014).

The majority of these studies use only the quantitative data available from Twitter, rather than qualitatively analyzing the content of specific Tweets. A key exception is Mitchell et al. (2013), which looks at happiness between states and urban areas within the United States and compares their sentiment analysis results to several other indicators of well-being, such as Gallup polls and gun violence rates. One of their more interesting findings was that areas with higher numbers of Tweets per capita tend to have less positive sentiment. They also correlated happiness from sentiment analysis with census data and found a strong correlation between cities with a higher percentage of white, married, higher-income residents and cities with higher happiness scores (Mitchell et al. 2013). Bertrand et al. (2013) conduct a sentiment analysis to Tweets at a much finer level of geographic detail, to explore how sentiment varies across different areas of New York City and changes over time.

A related stream of research evaluates Twitter and other social media venues as a potential tool of public engagement. Schweitzer (2014) finds evidence that transit agencies engaging more actively with other Twitter users, as opposed to simply blasting out information without the potential for a dynamic dialogue, experienced a significantly improved level of Twitter discourse surrounding public transit. Evans-Cowley and Griffin (2012) evaluate tweets and other online microblog forums in the development of the Austin, Texas (USA) Strategic Mobility Plan. The authors conclude that microblogging can be used to stimulate engagement from a more expansive public than typical of conventional forums and effectively measure sentiment and public opinion. However, public officials struggled to turn the reams of information into "stories that could resonate with decision makers" (p.97). Lòpez and Zaragoza (2015) examine a similar planning process in Mexico City, reaching similar conclusions regarding its potential value. Lastly, our own research has analyzed the potential and pitfalls of using Twitter data in a variety of local urban contexts and found promise for the methodology (Hollander et al. 2016).

Conclusion

Back to Washington Square Park and the proposed koi pond. Armed with an urban social listening approach, community engagement takes on a very different form. Instead of planners spending massive resources attempting to corral people into public meetings where they are not able to offer meaningful input, where the basic structure of the event might even result in invalid responses, where any input is unlikely to be generalizable to the broader 12 million users of the park annually, the planners reverse the directionality by listening to what users and visitors to the park know about, care about, and how they live their lives.

A review of publicly available Twitter and Instagram posts shows park usage trends, when people are spending time in the northwest corner (where the koi pond is proposed) and what are they doing (to the extent that they are posting about their activities). A survey of Flickr posts shows how the northwest corner of the park is photographed, a proxy for what people are finding meaningful and important about that part of the park. Mobile phone data tracks people's movements around the park, how they enter and exit, where they go before or after. Google and publicly available Facebook searches reveal the existence of hundreds of social groups (both formal and informal) that are built around using the park, a systematic content analysis of posts reveals opinions about the current park amenities and needs.

In this alternative universe, we can imagine that the insights from urban social listening at Washington Square Park speaks louder than the angry residents protesting at a public meeting might. The city planners begin to understand how the park is functioning, how that northwest corner is being used, and the design proposed is based on all of that human data. The final design presents an informed and educated picture of what a koi pond at Washington Square Park ought to look like, based on multiple data sources, valid, reliable, and generalizable. Certainly not without their limitations, not all social media is fully representative of a local population, not everyone has a mobile phone. But in sum, this urban social listening represents a sea change in the practice of urban planning. A chance to embrace the vast data sources available to enhance and improve the planning and design process.

In our analysis, there remains a need to open and transparent government, for which public meetings remain an essential component. But instead of relying on those meetings to be the place where planners and designers learn from people, those meetings instead become a place where the major investment of social listening, processing, and design is communicated back to the public for validation. Instead of presenting three designs for possible koi ponds, the presentation becomes an expression of the public will. An imperfect one, of course. No amount of Twitter posts and Google search data can fully capture people's opinions on a topic. Central to that problem is that people have competing opinions, competing values, and competing agendas. Planners and designers can only attempt to express the conflicts inherent in those conflicts and propose a vision of the future that reflects common group and shared values. It is that vision which should be field tested in a public forum, where protest, questioning, and interrogation are invited. It is only that kind of advanced vision, built on urban social listening and the expertise of the designer/planner that should be tested, not the naïve three versions of a possible koi pond that is today, unfortunately, common practice. Making this change is possible and can reorient community engagement in profound ways. For those ordinary public meetings that happen in American every day, an embrace of urban social listening can make them extraordinary. For real estate developers, the potential for urban social listening is to gain constructive and valuable insights to make their projects better, fit the needs of a community, and ameliorate the likelihood for resistance – altogether more people-centered.

CASE STUDY: Mosaic on the Riverway

Project Background

The Mosaic on the Riverway (See 12–5) in Boston sits near the boundaries of the Longwood Medical Area (LMA) and the Mission Hill neighborhoods of Boston (see Table 5.1). The LMA includes the medical facilities of Brigham and Women's Hospital, Beth Israel Deaconess Medical Center, Dana Farber Cancer Institute, Joslin Diabetes Center, and others as well as the academic institutions of Simmons College, Emmanuel College, Mass College of Pharmacy, Mass College of Art, Harvard Medical School, Harvard Dental School, and more (Boston Planning & Development Agency, n.d.) (See Figures 5.12, 5.13, 5.14, 5.15, and 5.16). The LMA and the Mosaic are adjacent to the Riverway section of the Emerald Necklace Park system in Boston (hence the name, Mosaic on the Riverway). While not

Table 5.1 Mosaic on the Riverway Boston, Massachusetts 2017 Winner.

Location	Boston, MA Longwood Medical Area neighborhood
Developer(s)	Roxbury Tenants of Harvard (RTH) (non-profit) Brigham and Women's Hospital (non-profit)
Landowner(s)	95-year ground lease from the State (DMH)
Year Opened	Fall 2016
Housing Type	145 units of housing • 42 market rate condominiums • 43 affordable condominiums 120% AMI • 60 affordable rental apartments 60% AMI
People-centered Aspects	• Non-luxury housing • Daycare, community resource • Public playground • *Transit proximity*
People-centered Process	Site Selection

Financing	• LIHTC
	• State funds
	• Bank of America Construction funding
	• MHP (Massachusetts housing partnership) with $2.1 million in long-term financing
	• $6 million from the City of Boston,
	  – including nearly $2 million in housing linkage funds created by Brigham Building for the Future,
	  – nearly $3 million provided by the Department of Neighborhood Development (DND), and
	  – $1 million from the Neighborhood Housing Trust

(by Nicole Stephens)

marketed as a transit-oriented development, the Mosaic is .3 miles from various stops on the Mass Bay Transportation Authority's (MBTA) Green Line E Branch and .6 miles from stops on the D Branch. In the following section, the story of how this project was conceived and developed will be presented, with a focus on the site selection process.

Site Selection Dimensions

The site was developed by the tenant-controlled and local non-profit Roxbury Tenants of Harvard (RTH) with aid and assistance from state agencies, the city of Boston, Partner's Healthcare, and Brigham and Women's Hospital (BWH). RTH

Figure 5.12 The Mosaic and Neighboring Parking Garage. Courtesy of Uma Edulbehram.

Figure 5.13 The Mosaic from Fenwood Road. Courtesy of Uma Edulbehram.

was founded in 1969 and, upon completion of the Mosaic, owns and operates over 1,000 units of housing including a 775 rental unit building across from the Mosaic (Roxbury Tenants of Harvard 2010 p. 2) (See Table 5.2). They are an established neighborhood institution known for their advocacy around affordability, explicit in their mission, "is to insure [sic] community participation in

Figure 5.14   The Mosaic from the Riverway. Courtesy of Uma Edulbehram.

Figure 5.15   The Riverway, a Part of the Emerald Necklace. Courtesy of Uma Edulbehram.

decision-making" (Roxbury Tenants of Harvard 2010.). Throughout the site selection process, RTH worked with numerous neighborhood institutions to bring this development to fruition.

The development is situated on what used to be Massachusetts Mental Health Center and the land is under a ninety-five-year ground lease from the Massachusetts' Department of Mental Health to Brigham, RTC is a sub-tenant. Affordable housing was a central component of this development and to

Figure 5.16 Map of Longwood area where the Mosaic on the Riverway stands. Courtesy of Uma Edulbehram.

Table 5.2 Unit mix at project.

Unit Mix					
Apartments		**Affordable Condominiums**		**Market Condominiums**	
Studios	0	Studios	0	Studios	5
One-Bedroom	6	One-Bedroom	9	One-Bedroom	26
Two-Bedrooms	48	Two-Bedrooms	29	Two-Bedrooms	11
Three-Bedrooms	6	Three-Bedrooms	5	Three-Bedrooms	0
Four-Bedrooms	0	Four-Bedrooms	0	Penthouse	0

guarantee this, BWH did not attribute a land value to the RTC residential parcel – essentially giving it to RTH for free (Roxbury Tenants of Harvard 2010 p. 33). Further, BWH contributed $3 million for pre-construction and construction costs and agreed to extend a letter of credit or guarantee a letter of credit for $2 million in financing for the building to state and city agencies (ibid p. 33). Additional major sources of funding included low-income housing tax credits (LIHTC) and $6 million from various city of Boston agencies for the $63 million development (Mosaic on the Riverway 2017). Many different institutions (government and non-profit) came together to sponsor scores of public meetings and boosting community power to make this development happen. Through the site selection, they were motivated to situate affordable housing near good, well-paying jobs – advancing key local and economic goals for the community.

People-Centered Components

The Mosaic includes sixty affordable rentals, forty-three affordable condominiums, and forty-two market rate condominiums totaling 145 units of housing with 71% designated as affordable. The affordable rental units are available to people making up to 60% area median income (AMI) and the affordable condos are set to 120% of AMI. With 77 two-bedroom units and 11 three-bedroom units, the project created affordable housing for families (Mosaic on the Riverway 2017). The rental units make up floors 2, 3, 4, and 5 with the condominiums occupying floors 6–10, and a daycare on the first floor of the building (ibid). It was an intentional choice to intersperse the market and affordable condo units on each of the floors. There is no poor floor akin to New York City's infamous "poor door" development (Licea 2016).

Additional people-centered aspects of the Mosaic development included a childcare facility (Figure 5.17), a community driven amenity. Encompassing the first floor, the roughly 9,000 square foot facility serves nearly 100 children and is run through the YMCA of Boston (Boston Housing Development Honored for

Figure 5.17 Early childhood education center at the Mosaic on the Riverway project. Courtesy of Uma Edulbehram.

Affordable and Workforce Housing from Urban Land Institute 2017). A public playground and a variety of pedestrian paths are other people-centered components that benefit the neighborhood and building residents (See Figures 5.18 and 5.19). Finally, in terms of sustainability, the Mosaic development meets LEED Silver, Energy Star, and Enterprise Green Community standards (ibid).

Figure 5.18   People-centered component, public seating. Courtesy of Uma Edulbehram.

Figure 5.19   People-centered component, playground. Courtesy of Uma Edulbehram.

Case Takeaways

Non-profits by design are concerned with people and they can provide capital, expertise, and other supports to bolster the success of a development both during construction and after construction programmatically. Hospitals and colleges/universities are large non-profits that can bolster people-centered development goals. They, like government, are not seeking to maximize their profits but rather for a place to reinvest in their mission and/or or the community that they serve. The Mosaic site and the multiple non-profit parties interested in its success were able to situate housing near a large job center and helped to invest in the neighborhood. The partnerships between non-profits at Mosaic and at other sites can consolidate resources and services for people to improve development.

Bibliography

Antonelli, F., Azzi, M., Balduini, M., Ciuccarelli, P., Valle, E.D., and Larcher, R. (2014). City sensing: visualising mobile and social data about a city scale event. In *Proceedings of the 2014 International Working Conference on Advanced Visual Interfaces*. May 2014: 337–338. ACM.

Arnstein, S.R. (1969). A ladder of citizen participation. *Journal of the American Institute of Planners* 35 (4): 216–224. doi: 10.1080/01944366908977225.

Balduini, M., Della Valle, E., Dell'Aglio, D., Tsytsarau, M., Palpanas, T., and Confalonieri, C. (2013). *Social listening of city scale events using the streaming linked data framework. The Semantic Web–ISWC 2013*. 1–16. Springer Berlin Heidelberg.

Beauregard, R.A. (2006). *When America Became Suburban*. University of Minnesota Press.

Bertrand, K.Z., Bialik, M., Virdee, K., Gros, A., and Bar-Yam, Y. (2013). *Sentiment in new york city: A high resolution spatial and temporal view. arXiv preprint arXiv:1308.5010.*

Bollen, J., Mao, H., and Pepe, A. (2011). Modeling public mood and emotion: Twitter sentiment and socio-economic phenomena. In *ICWSM*. July 2011.

Boston Fair Housing (n.d.) *1970s–Present: restriction of multi-family zoning.* [online]. https://www.bostonfairhousing.org/timeline/1970s-present-Local-Land_use-Regulations-2.html.

Boston Planning & Development Agency (n.d.) *2021 Income, asset, and price limits.* [online]. http://www.bostonplans.org/housing/income,-asset,-and-price-limits (accessed July 2, 2022).

Bronin, S. (2021). Zoning by a thousand cuts. *Pepperdine Law Review* 50. doi: 10.2139/ssrn.3792544.

Caro. (1975). *The Power Broker: Robert Moses and the Fall of New York*. New York: Vintage Books.

Domanski, B. and Krzysztof, G. (2010). Multiplier effects in local and regional development. *Quaestiones Geographica* 29 (2).

Duggan, M. (2015). *The demographics of social media users*. [online] Pew Research Center: Internet, Science & Tech. https://www.pewinternet.org/2015/08/19/the-demographics-of-social-media-users (accessed July 2, 2022).

Evans-Cowley, J. and Griffin, G. (2012). Microparticipation with social media for community engagement in transportation planning. *Transportation Research Record: Journal of the Transportation Research Board* 2307: 90–98.

Evans-Cowley, J. and Hollander, J. (2010). The new generation of public participation: internet-based participation tools. *Planning Practice & Research* 25 (3): 397–408.

Frumkin, H. (2002). Urban sprawl and public health. *Public Health Reports* 117 (3): 201–2017. doi: 10.1093/phr/117.3.201.

Fujisaka, T., Lee, R., and Sumiya, K. (2010). Discovery of user behavior patterns from geo-tagged micro-blogs. In *Proceedings of the 4th International Conference on Uniquitous Information Management and Communication*, pp. 1–10.

Gordon, E. (2016). *Accelerating Public Engagement: A Roadmap for Local Government*. Creative Commons Non-Commercial Share Alike 4.0 License (International).

Gordon, E., Schirra, S., and Hollander, J.B. (2011). Immersive planning: a conceptual model for designing public participation with new technologies. *Environment and Planning B: Planning and Design* 38 (3): 505–519. doi: 10.1068/b37013.

Gordon, J. (2013). Comparative geospatial analysis of Twitter sentiment data during the 2008 and 2012 US Presidential elections. *PhD diss.*, University of Oregon.

Gough, A., Hunter, R.F., Ajao, O. et al. (2017). Tweet for behavior change: using social media for the dissemination of public health messages. *JMIR Public Health and Surveillance* 3 (1): e14. doi: 10.2196/publichealth.6313.

Gross, J. (2007). Community benefits agreements: definitions, values, and legal enforceability. *Journal of Affordable Housing & Community Development Law* [online] 17 (1/2): 35–58. http://www.jstor.org/stable/25782803 [accessed November 8, 2022].

Hirt, S. (2015). *Zoned in the USA: The Origins and Implications of American Land-use Regulation*. Ithaca: Cornell University Press.

Hollander, J. (2011). Approaching an ideal: using technology to apply collaborative rationality to urban planning processes. *Planning Practice and Research* 26 (5): 587–596.

Hollander, J. (2012). Intelligent participation: engaging citizens through a framework of multiple intelligences. *Community Development* 43 (3): 346–360.

Hollander, J. (2021). Rethinking digital community engagement. In: *Masterlin Leah*. New York: Columbia University Books on Architecture and Urbanism: *Digital Urbanisms*.

Hollander, J.B. (2009). *Polluted, and Dangerous: America's Worst Abandoned Properties and What Can Be Done about Them*. Burlington, VT: University of Vermont Press.

Hollander, J.B. (2011). *Sunburnt Cities: The Great Recession, Depopulation and Urban Planning in the American Sunbelt*. London and New York: Routledge.

Hollander, J.B., Graves, E., Renski, H., Foster-Karim, C., Wiley, A., and Das, D. (2016). *Urban Social Listening: Potential and Pitfalls of Using Social Media Data in Studying Cities*. New York: Palgrave Macmillan.

Hollander, J., Kirkwood, N., and Gold, J. (2010). *Principles of Brownfield Regeneration: Cleanup, Design, and Reuse of Derelict Land*. Washington, DC: Island Press.

Knapp, C.E. and Hollander, J.B. (2012). Exploring the potential for integrating community benefits agreements into brownfield redevelopment projects. In: *Reclaiming Brownfields: A Comparative Analysis of Adaptive Reuse of Contaminated Properties* (Global Urban Book Series, Michigan State University) (ed. C. Jackson-Elmoore, R.C. Hula, and L.A. Reese). London: Ashgate.

Kunstler, J.H. (1994). *The Geography of Nowhere: The Rise and Decline of America's Man-made Landscape*. New York: Simon & Schuster.

Lee, C. (2020). Metropolitan sprawl measurement and its impacts on commuting trips and road emissions. *Transportation Research Part D: Transport and Environment* 82: 102329.

Licea, M. (2016). *'Poor door' tenants of luxury tower reveal the financial apartheid within*. [online] New York Post. https://nypost.com/2016/01/17/poor-door-tenants-reveal-luxury-towers-financial-apartheid (accessed November 8, 2022).

López-Ornelas, E. and Zaragoza, N.M. (2015). Social media participation: a narrative way to help urban planners. In *International Conference on Social Computing and Social Media* (pp. 48–54). Springer International Publishing.

Lovelace, R., Malleson, N., Harland, K., and Birkin, M. (2014). *Geotagged tweets to inform a spatial interaction model: a case study of museums. arXiv preprint arXiv:1403.5118*.

MacEachren, A.M., Robinson, A., Jaiswal, A., Pezanowski, S., Savelyev, A., Blanford, J., and Mitra, P. (2011). Geo-twitter analytics: applications in crisis management. *25th International Cartographic Conference*.

Mearns, G., Simmonds, R., Richardson, R., Turner, M., Watson, P., and Missier, P. (2014). Tweet my street: a cross-disciplinary collaboration for the analysis of local Twitter data. *Future Internet* 6 (2): 378–396.

Mitchell, L., Frank, M.R., Harris, K.D., Dodds, P.S., and Danforth, C.M. (2013). The geography of happiness: Connecting Twitter sentiment and expression, demographics, and objective characteristics of place. *PloS one* 8 (5): e64417.

Mosaic on the Riverway (2017). *Presented at the Urban Land Institute Housing Conference*, September. https://housingconference.uli.org/wp-content/uploads/sites/101/2017/07/4.-Hahnel-Mosaic-ULI-Community-Serving-Real-Estate.pdf.

O'Connor, B., Balasubramanyan, R., Routledge, B.R., and Smith, N.A. (2010). From tweets to polls: linking text sentiment to public opinion time series. *ICWSM* 11: 122–129.

Pew Research Center (2015). *Demographics of Social Media Users in 2015*. August. https://www.pewinternet.org/2015/08/19/the-demographics-of-social-media-users (accessed March 21, 2019).

Philadelphia 2035 (n.d.) *Citywide vision summary*. [online]. https://www.phila2035. org/citywide-vision (accessed September 20, 2022).

Poorthuis, A. and Zook, M. (2014). Artists and bankers and hipsters, Oh My! Mapping tweets in the New York Metropolitan Region. *Cityscape: A Journal of Policy Development and Research* 16 (2): 169–172.

Presented at the Urban Land Institute Housing Conference (2017). *Mosaic on the Riverway*. [online]. https://housingconference.uli.org/wp-content/uploads/ sites/101/2017/07/4.-Hahnel-Mosaic-ULI-Community-Serving-Real-Estate.pdf (accessed September 20, 2022).

Quercia, D., Ellis, J., Capra, L., and Crowcroft, J. (2012). Tracking gross community happiness from tweets. *Proceedings of the ACM 2012 conference on Computer Supported Cooperative Work* February 2012: 965–968. ACM.

Roxbury Tenants of Harvard (2010). *Development plan for PDA #76 RTH residential building*. [online]. http://www.bostonplans.org/documents/zoning/planned-development-areas/pda-76-development-plan-for-pda-76-rth-residential (accessed September 20, 2022).

Saito, L. and Truong, J. (2014). The L.A. Live community benefits agreement. *Urban Affairs Review* 51 (2): 263–289. doi: 10.1177/1078087414527064.

Salkin, P. and Lavine, A. (2008). Understanding community benefits agreements: equitable development, social justice and other considerations for developers, municipalities and community organizations. [online] *papers.ssrn.com*. https:// ssrn.com/abstract=1272795 (accessed November 8, 2022).

Schweitzer, L. (2014). Planning and social media: a case study of public transit and stigma on Twitter. *Journal of the American Planning Association* 80 (3): 218–238.

Sinnenberg, L., Buttenheim, A.M., Padrez, K. et al. (2017). Twitter as a tool for health research: a systematic review. *American Journal of Public Health* 107 (1): e1–e8. doi: 10.2105/ajph.2016.303512.

Stone, K. (1997). Impact of the Wal-Mart Phenomenon on Rural Communities. *Proceedings of the Farm Foundation*. Chicago, IL.

US EPA,OLEM (2019). *Overview of EPA's brownfields program | US EPA*. [online] US EPA. https://www.epa.gov/brownfields/overview-epas-brownfields-program (accessed July 2, 2022).

Vlachokyriakos, V., Crivellaro, C., Le Dantec, C.A. et al. (2016). Digital civics. In: *Proceedings of the 2016 CHI Conference Extended Abstracts on Human Factors in Computing Systems*. doi: 10.1145/2851581.2886436.

Wallace, D.A. (2004). *Urban Planning/my Way*. American Planning Association.

Wojcik, S. and Hughes, A. (2019). Sizing up Twitter users. *Pew Research Center*. April.

Wu, W. and Gaubatz, P.R. (2013). *The Chinese City*. Abingdon, Oxon and New York, NY: Routledge.

www.bostonplans.org (2017). *Boston housing development honored for affordable and workforce housing from Urban Land Institute | Boston planning & development agency*. [online]. http://www.bostonplans.org/news-calendar/news-updates/2017/10/4/boston-housing-development-honored-for-affordable (accessed September 20, 2022).

Yang, J., Brandon, P.S., and Sidwell, A.C. (2008). *Smart and Sustainable Built Environments*. John Wiley & Sons.

Yuen, B. (2011). Centenary paper: urban planning in Southeast Asia: perspective from Singapore. *Town Planning Review* 82 (2): 145–168. doi: 10.3828/tpr.2011.12.

6

Site Analysis and Planning

Earlier in the book, we introduced some of the rules and regulations utilized by local governments to control land development. We spent a lot of time on zoning and briefly mentioned building codes and subdivision control regulations. This chapter examines the next sequential step in the real estate development process after the identification of a location: analyzing and planning for how the site will be developed; which requires a close review of those many rules, laws, and regulations that govern land development.

This is a step that needs to be done before finalizing a site location in order to ensure that the entire "program" (those requirements of a client or future end user) can be satisfied on the given site. Ideally, such analysis is integrated into the decision-making process described in the previous chapter, whereby each possible site's advantages and disadvantages are weighed. While the implementation of the site analysis and planning stage happens next, it needs to commence well before the site is acquired for development.

`The program drives all site analysis and planning; it is essentially the mission of this stage. If the developer is seeking to build single-family homes on a cul-de-sac or renovate an empty mill, that ultimate end use will organize the work at this point. The use of the site will be restricted by existing zoning of the property. As discussed earlier in the book, every property in just about every city in America (Houston, Texas is an exception) has been assigned a use category, for example Single Family Residential or Medium Density Office. For each use category, by right uses are enumerated in the zoning ordinance and a broader range of uses are allowed by some form of special permit or request. The first step in site analysis is to determine what current zoning law allows by right or by special permit. As we have argued earlier, the framework of zoning does allow for exceptions, appeals, and revisions, particularly in response to major development proposals, but those all cost money and time and the site

Buildings for People: Responsible Real Estate Development and Planning, First Edition.
Justin B. Hollander and Nicole E. Stephens.
© 2023 John Wiley & Sons, Inc. Published 2023 by John Wiley & Sons, Inc.

analysis should begin by identifying what is possible regarding use without such legal and political maneuvers.

In addition to zoning, subdivision control regulations are critical in the site analysis stage to understand how a property can be broken up into smaller lots. Most localities severely constrain the subdivision process and require that each lot have a reasonable length of frontage – that linear amount of feet which the lot lies along a street. Local governments are seeking to avoid the construction of lots that are in the shapes of flags, whereby each has only ten to twelve feet of frontage, just wide enough for a driveway. Typical frontage requirements run around 100 or 200 feet in the United States. For a single-family housing development, such subdivision is essential to be able for the developer to sell off individual house lots. Subdivision may also be important in other mixed-use developments where multiple owners are expected, each with their own lots and frontage.

Less common but still important local, state, and federal government regulations that may need to be included in a site analysis include wetlands rules, coastal or floodplain regulations, other environmental guidance, affordable housing requirements, form/bulk/height/landscaping restrictions, and siting requirements that require buffers from abutters. Environmental rules will vary from place to place and will demand close review and the services of environmental professionals to ensure full compliance. A site analysis might identify constraints on the site, consider abutting uses, and highlight possible places for locating structures, roads, and utilities.

Conducting a Site Analysis

A critical step in conducting a site analysis is an in-person visit. While online maps and Google Streetview can be invaluable tools, there is no substitute for walking around the property, checking out the neighborhood, and casually talking to neighbors or passersby. People who know an area well, just might be willing to share their stories and sometimes even tell secrets about a site or the immediate neighborhood. The general sense of safety and security of a place can be gauged by physical inspection of properties, are there bars in windows, are there substantial gates or fences? Is there evidence of ongoing criminal activity, signs of gang activity, vandalism, or graffiti? Do people you see seem relaxed and open or tense and guarded? What do they have to say about the neighborhood?

A visual inspection of the condition of buildings, landscaping, garbage/recycling storage can reveal a lot about how well current property owners care for their own investments. Is the paint peeling on exterior walls, are porches falling apart, are hedges being trimmed, are there dead trees around, is trash overflowing from dumpsters? No answers to these questions or others posed in this chapter should necessarily disqualify a property from consideration but should feed into the overall site analysis and plan for a site.

The in-person site reconnaissance can help a developer understand the context of a property in a way that is impossible if done remotely from an office. By visiting, a developer can appreciate the relationship between the property and the larger neighborhood, the sense of scale and proportion that is harder to assess from a computer screen. Environmental hazards can be better understood first-hand, whether that means evidence of flooding through stains on buildings, or the condition of wetlands, or evidence of dumping on or near the site, or suspicious oil or other toxic smells. Even environmentally benign odors related to industrial processes or accumulating refuse will be a factor in analyzing a site. Likewise, the soothing fragrance of nearby flower nurseries or neighbors who grow stunning gardens can be considered a key amenity in a site analysis. Visiting a site also allows for a developer to assess noise pollution, the considerations and tools for such analysis follows in the next section.

Noise Pollution

Walking around a potential development site and listening carefully, can be an important first step in a site analysis. While a map may have shown a nearby highway, how loud is it at the site? Maybe an airport is close by, but are planes flying low overhead? (See Figure 6.1). What about power lines, the noise they generate may be substantial. Are there restaurants or bars nearby which regularly host live music performances? What about outdoor sporting events? (See Yuen 2014).

A noise mapping assessment (also known as a noise impact assessment) is a systematic collection of various possible sources of noise pollution, quantified, and mapped in the vicinity of a development site (Lee et al. 2008; Bunn and Zannin 2015). (See Figure 6.2). Part of this assessment is to collect baseline data through the measurement of noises at different times of the day, days of the week, and locations within the site. Then, the analyst makes reasonable projections as to how the proposed development might exacerbate those noises.

Part of analyzing a site for noise pollution involves a close look at the potential for noise attenuation remedies to be put in place. For example, introducing speed reduction requirements on nearby roadways, erecting noise barriers at or near the perimeter of the site, or working with public authorities to curtail or eliminate the sources of loud noises (Lee et al. 2008). The noise mapping assessment then

Figure 6.1 Plane flying over residential London neighborhood approaching London Heathrow Airport. Adrian Pingstone / Wikimedia Commons / Public Domain.

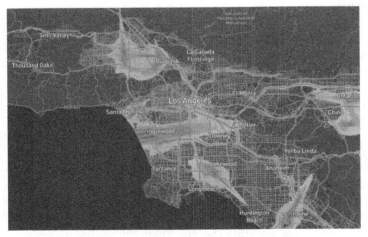

Figure 6.2 Transportation noise density map of greater Los Angeles, California. Map and data from Bureau of Transportation Statistics/Screenshot by Uma Edulbehram.

explores how the noise attenuation measures might reduce noise levels. Ultimately, this kind of assessment can estimate how many people in a given site might be impacted by loud noises, just another factor in assessing the conditions of a given site (Lee et al. 2008).

Air Quality

Air pollution can impact prospects for a site in a number of ways. First, high levels of pollution based on external factors like a nearby factory may make a program for a site impossible. For example, the air pollution emanating from that factory may make outdoor recreational spaces unattractive for a proposed resort development. Second, air pollution is often linked to foul smells and smog, olfactory and visual blights that can limit the appeal of a development for future occupants (see Figure 6.3). Third, the proposed uses on the site themselves might just generate enough air pollution that given the topography and geography of the surrounding area could trigger local, state, or even federal oversight making the project untenable.

For all of these reasons, it is essential for the real estate development team to undertake a site analysis that assesses the regional air quality conditions, the microclimate of a site to be able to model how nearby pollutants might impact air quality on the site, and to model how the proposed use of the site might contribute to broader air pollution patterns in the region.

The first step to understanding regional air quality conditions is to review how national, state, or provincial government agencies classify the region where the site is located. In the United States, the federal Environmental Protection Agency (EPA) monitors air pollution in partnership with states, tribes, and local governments and makes a determination whether a given region is in attainment with the various air pollution standards (See Figure 6.4). If not, the EPA designates that

Figure 6.3 Air pollution in Tehran, Iran, 2019. By Mehr News Agency, CC BY 4.0. https://commons.wikimedia.org/w/index.php?curid=85043620.

region as being in nonattainment and imposes a number of stringent controls on new development and infrastructure (Steiner and Butler 2007). Large swaths of the East and West Coast, as well as numerous major population centers throughout the rest of the United States are presently in that nonattainment category. Depending on the proposed program of use, this nonattainment designation may or may not be an impediment – here the services of an environmental attorney can be useful to navigate the byzantine rules and regulations around state and federal air pollution.

It's one thing if your site is located in a nonattainment county, it is another for the site's immediate microclimate to literally be polluted. To ascertain that

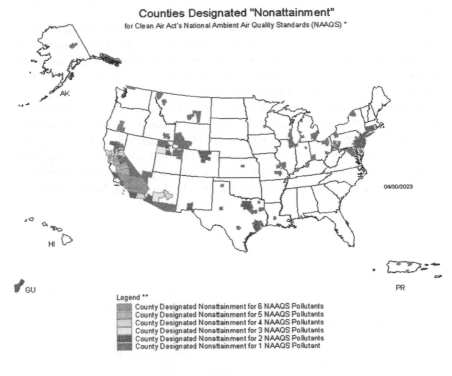

Counties Designated "Nonattainment"
for Clean Air Act's National Ambient Air Quality Standards (NAAQS) *

04/30/2023

AK

HI

GU

PR

Legend **

☐ County Designated Nonattainment for 6 NAAQS Pollutants
☐ County Designated Nonattainment for 5 NAAQS Pollutants
☐ County Designated Nonattainment for 4 NAAQS Pollutants
☐ County Designated Nonattainment for 3 NAAQS Pollutants
☐ County Designated Nonattainment for 2 NAAQS Pollutants
☐ County Designated Nonattainment for 1 NAAQS Pollutant

* The National Ambient Air Quality Standards (NAAQS) are health standards for Carbon Monoxide, Lead (1978 and 2008), Nitrogen Dioxide, 8-hour Ozone (2008), Particulate Matter (PM-10 and PM-2.5 (1997, 2006 and 2012), and Sulfur Dioxide.(1971 and 2010)

** Included in the counts are counties designated for NAAQS and revised NAAQS pollutants. Revoked 1-hour (1979) and 8-hour Ozone (1997) are excluded. Partial counties, those with part of the county designated nonattainment and part attainment, are shown as full counties on the map.

Figure 6.4 US counties designated by the US Environmental Protection Agency as in nonattainment for the Clean Air Act's National Ambient Air Quality Standards. US Environmental Protection Agency 2022.

requires some data collection and analysis. An inventory of surrounding uses is a good first step. When approaching this task, it is useful to consider the different sources of air pollution: point, line, and area (Blond et al. 2017). Point sources are the usual suspects: factories, airports, and power generation plants. Line sources are those transportation systems like roads and rails that generate linear pollution. Area sources, also known as non-point sources, encompass all other ways in which air pollution is generated from residential, agricultural, or commercial areas. For these area sources, the individual home or farm might only release an insignificant amount of pollution, but collectively their impact can be sizable (Blond et al. 2017). In one study of a city in France, researchers found that these area sources were the biggest sources of air pollution in the region and they were most intense in the most densely developed parts of a city (Le Boennec and Salladarré 2017). These area sources can be so diffuse and comprehensive that they can seriously impact a local ecosystem's ability to purify the air (Xu et al. 2016).

Interestingly, research has shown that air pollution has little bearing on property values (Cavailhes 2005; Le Boennec and Salladarré 2017). Those area sources of pollution mean jobs and economic opportunities, those linear sources mean roads and rails. These amenities are attractive and people want to be where the action is. Figure 6.4 shows that many of those counties in nonattainment are some of the most desirable (and expensive) places to live in the United States. While there are severe deleterious impacts on human health from air pollution, real estate developers will rarely avoid building at a location only because air quality may be compromised.

If a given site has sizable numbers of any of these air pollution sources in close proximity, further analysis is warranted. Civil and environmental engineers are trained to collect and analyze data on these sources to estimate the microclimate on a site. One tool widely used is the Air Pollution Model (TAPM) which considers not only air pollution sources in an area (point, line, and area source), but also meteorological conditions (Hurley et al. 2005; Carnevale et al. 2017). TAPM and other similar tools look to measure and project impacts of pollutants like CO_2, Lead, NO_2, particulate matter (PM), Ozone (O_3), and SO_2 (Steiner and Butler 2007). These types of models can estimate the approximate shape of pollutant plumes and to advise a real estate developer around the risks that external factors might have on the air quality on a site.

The same models can take information from a developer about their proposed plan for a site and combine that with baseline conditions to assess how the project might impact the surrounding area. For a modest subdivision of single-family homes, this is a non-issue. But if the proposed project involves high levels of emissions, e.g. a gas-fired power plant or a bus repair depot, then advanced air quality modeling, like a TAPM, can project how the project might generate new air pollution off-site. Because local topography and hydrological conditions are baked into a TAPM model (due to how meteorology reflects those conditions) each site will generate a different air pollution footprint. Put another way: even the most noxious use can have only minimal impact on surrounding air quality if topography, vegetation, hydrology, and other meteorological conditions are favorable. A thorough analysis of air quality impacts at this early stage can limit the likelihood for future costs, complaints, and fines if a developer's project becomes a major source for air pollution for a region.

Transportation/Mobility

Examining the infrastructure surrounding and serving a site is critical, especially water, sewer, and electricity. Fortunately, those services – if present – are fairly fixed and a cursory review of utilities' track records, finances, and quality performance may be sufficient at this stage in site analysis. What is much more complex and deserving of a section here in this chapter is with respect to the transportation infrastructure that serves a site. Without adequate roads, transit, rail, or ports, a site will be isolated, and any proposed development may fail.

Any site analysis for transportation will need to begin with questions around road frontage. Does the property either abut or include public roadways? If so, what kinds of roadways? Planners and engineers classify roads into a hierarchy, from highest capacity to lowest: principal arterial, minor arterial, collector streets, and local streets (Steiner and Butler 2007). For each, numerous standards are published to consider the capacity of the roadway, the expected flow of traffic, and the width/configuration of the right-of-way. These roads are distinct from the highways and freeways that have limited access and carry much of a given country's freight.

Freight also arrives at a site by rail, air, and water. For commercial and industrial developments, access to these transportation networks will be critical, for residential proximity to such facilities may be considered a dis-amenity. A site analysis should consider access to the kinds of goods and materials needed, but a cargo airport might also be close to a passenger airport and improve mobility for future residents in a proposed housing development.

After cataloguing the transportation infrastructure nearby or on a site, making rough assessments of the capacity of each and the overall ability of that transportation system to meet the needs of the program, the next step is a more systematic analysis. Like the air pollution modeling described earlier, transportation planners and engineers use advanced computer models to project two things: (1) how a proposed site development will impact the surrounding transportation network, and (2) how well that network, combined with transportation improvements on the site (as part of the proposed development) can provide for the mobility of users. For both, a site plan is required for a proposed development that conceptually illustrates the use and transportation infrastructure for the site. In this plan, the types of roads (arterial, collector, local, etc.), the pedestrian and bike network, and any public transit enhancements would all be included. Depending on the nature, size, and scale of a proposed development, major public infrastructure investments may be needed, including major roads, transit line extensions, or even highway spurs. At this site analysis and planning stage, with likely little in the way of guarantees for such public support in hand, the developer is only seeking to make rudimentary estimations on the kinds of transportation system that may be installed on a site, with plenty of caveats around unknowns.

With such a site plan in hand, a consulting planner or engineer should be enlisted to conduct basic modeling on the two above analytical steps. The travel demand model provides a developer with an estimate of how many trips their proposed project will generate both on the site and off-site (ICMA 2000). A typical travel demand model begins with data on land use (from the developer's site plan and from existing data provided by a local government or vendor), socio-economic data (may be available from a local government or vendor), and the existing street network and historic trip counts. The model then estimates the total number of trips and how they might be distributed by mode, e.g., car, bike, walking, or public transit. Then, the model assigns trips to each of the road, transit, bike, or pedestrian segments of the network.

The site plan can then be adjusted and the model re-run as part of an iterative process of accomplishing a range of mobility goals for users of the proposed development and for managing and minimizing traffic impacts off-site. Complaints around possible new car or truck traffic generation can be a hurdle for a development project and this kind of modeling can show how adjustments were made to the site plan to reduce those impacts.[1]

Car traffic off-site can be drastically reduced at this stage through the development of bike and pedestrian infrastructure, public transit, and ride sharing services. As highlighted above, what matters most in the mobility realm are trips and modal split. How many times will a person have to travel from point A to point B and how will they travel, car, bike, walk, or public transit? The installation of bike infrastructure, lanes, sharrows, routes that traverse a site and connect with bike networks off-site can attract riders. Noted Danish urban planner Jan Gehl (2010) helped Copenhagen introduce extensive bike infrastructure and witnessed first-hand how that resulted in a modal shift away from driving toward biking. Research around the pedestrian experience, by Gehl and others, likewise has shown that improving the public realm through high quality edges (see Figures 6.5 and 6.6), attention to key urban design patterns and shapes, a narrative

Figure 6.5 Tamarack Street in Washington D.C, exemplary of car friendly neighborhood. thisisbossi / Flickr / CC BY-SA 2.0.

Figure 6.6 Example of high quality street edge in Houston, Texas. Michael Barera, CC BY-SA 4.0, via Wikimedia Commons.

experience, and biophilic elements all contribute to shifting modal split toward more walking (Hollander and Sussman 2021; Sussman and Hollander 2021).

With governmental support, public transit can also support mobility within a site and connect users to a surrounding transit system, all reducing car trips. That can mean as little as a bus stop on the edge of a site all the way to installing a new transit line into a site and establishing multiple stations. Whatever the form, these kinds of public transit investments can be coupled with bike and ped infrastructure to reduce the number of times that users of the proposed site have to drive when they need to make a trip. It shifts the modal split away from driving and ultimately means less cars and less traffic both on and off-site.

There is another strategy that can shift modal split: ride sharing. While still relying on automobiles, research has shown that (especially younger) people are increasingly eschewing car ownership and instead relying on ped, bike, transit and ride sharing (Delbosc and Currie 2013; McDonald 2015). But these car-free folks need to be in places that are ped-bike-transit friendly, which puts pressure on the site plan to include that necessary infrastructure. This trend toward a car-free lifestyle is not always voluntarily in that low-income people tend to lack access to car ownership or a driver's license, making ride sharing, walking, biking, and transit requirements for mobility (Liu and Painter 2012).

Hydrology

Water occupies 71% of the surface of our planet, the oceans comprise 95.5 percent of the Earth's water, but on *terra firma* water is also quite ubiquitous and can represent a serious impediment to constructing building (US Geological Survey's Water Science School 2018). Analyzing a site has to include a thorough examination of all aspects of hydrology: rivers, streams, lakes, wetlands, and rainfall. Numerous federal laws, most notably the Clean Water Act, govern development activities regarding water, as do state and local regulations. But not every drop of water is the same and careful analysis can reveal to the extent that a site may or may not be suitable for development.

Rainfall is an important consideration in site analysis because that water that falls from the sky has to have a place to go. If a site is in a climatic zone with high levels of rainfall or regular acute storms, then the surface runoff from that rain can cause problem both on site and off site. Hack (2018) argues that developers and planners should develop site design strategies to ensure "zero net runoff" (p. 367) so no rainwater leaves a site to generate difficulties for neighbors. To do so requires a range of retention and absorption strategies which we will return to in Chapter 7, but in the site analysis stage the question is: in its current state, how is water managed from rainfall? Does it currently cause flooding or pooling on site? Does it currently flood abutting properties? Are there many pervious surfaces where water infiltrates into the ground and will the introduction of buildings and roads with their new impervious surfaces substantially change that current surface runoff pattern? Depending on the answers to those questions, a trained environmental scientist or engineer may need to be consulted to assess the feasibility and costs of those retention and absorption strategies that Hack (2018) recommends.

Ordinary and even heavy rain is one thing, but some areas have entire rivers and streams that run through them or are on a lake or sea. Variability is the size and extant of these water bodies, high and low tide, these are all major factors in a site analysis. A stream bed may be dry one day and flowing mightily the next. In the United States, the US Geological Survey can help: they produce comprehensive hydrological maps at a fine level of granularity (states and some localities also offer such spatial data) (See Figures 6.7–6.10).

These maps show the location of perhaps less visually obvious hydrological features: wetlands, riparian corridors, and floodplains. Wetlands can comprise

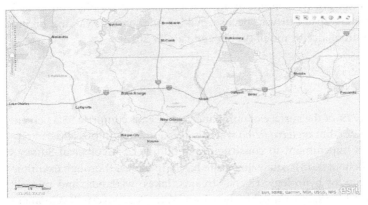

Figure 6.7 Map of Southern Louisiana. Courtesy of the United States Geological Survey.

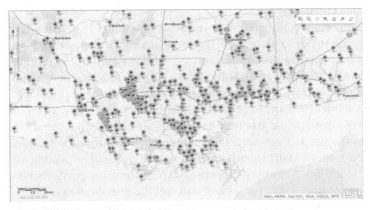

Figure 6.8 Map indicating sites of surface water. Courtesy of the United States Geological Survey

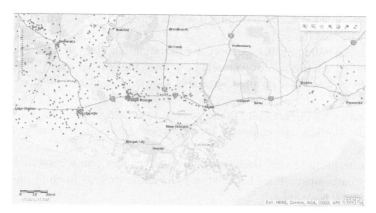

Figure 6.9 Map indicating sites of ground water. Courtesy of the United States Geological Survey.

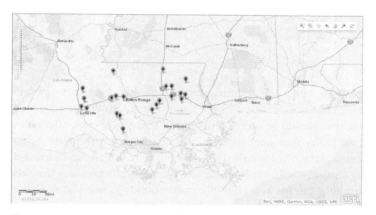

Figure 6.10 Map indicating atmospheric sites. Courtesy of the United States Geological Survey.

marshes, swamps, bogs, or fens, all highly protected by federal and state laws (Steiner and Butler 2007). That is not to say a developer cannot fill in a wetland; these laws simply regulate that filling and require building new wetlands at other locations – all at significant costs. Regarding floodplains, building within them may be legally possible, but the possibility of a rare flood event will translate to higher property insurance costs and can literally destroy an entire building (wiping out a developer's profits with it).

Experts have identified four key considerations for how to approach replacing and restoring wetlands:

First, based on local needs and limitations we should elucidate what the wetland is needed for.

Second, depending on the creation or restoration objective that is pursued and the local limitations it should be defined the scale at which wetland might be created or restored, so as site, subcatchment, catchment, or territory.

Third, when we pursue more than one objective, then, we should carefully study conflicts and compatibilities between creation or restoration objectives.

Fourth, according to the decisions taken at steps first and second and conflicts and compatibilities found at step third, the strategy to build the wetlands must be defined.

(Moreno-Mateos and Comin 2010, p. 2094)

These steps will help support an area's broader ecological health through a thoughtful, goal-oriented approach that manages conflicts with existing and proposed land uses.

Hazards

Flooding is one of the biggest hazards human settlements face the planet over and they are not a new phenomenon. But they are actually just one of numerous hazards that a site analysis should be on the lookout for. Site geology can offer clues to the potential of faults that may increase the chances of a property being impacted by an earthquake. Geology also tells us about soils, which can be a factor in how a building withstands an earthquake, but also generally provides insights into the suitability of a site for any kind of construction (e.g. soft clays). Other potential hazards around soils are erosion and sedimentation which can threaten the structural stability of buildings and infrastructure. Erosion can be caused over time by wind, ice, water, and human activity, while sedimentation results from the accumulation of sediment – largely from water sources (Steiner and Butler 2007). Thus, riverine and coastal locations are most susceptible to erosion and sedimentation (Steiner and Butler 2007) (see Figure 6.11). Landslides, sink holes, and subsidence are all also ground-related challenges and in some ways extreme forms of erosion, where soils and rocks give way to gravitational pull and threaten human life. Landscape, in particular, are most common in areas with steep slopes, that is changes in elevation in a close geography. Historically, builders have avoided these slopes whenever possible, simply due to the increased costs of building on hills. But in a locale with high land values, building structures on slopes might be cost effective, but the risks of landslides should be accounted for.

Figure 6.11 Instance of coastal erosion affecting residential real estate in Florida. paulbr75 / Pixabay.

Hurricanes, tornadoes, typhoons, tsunamis, and other strong storm systems represent a different type of hazard, where a site analysis might look for historic patterns of these storms or evidence of levees and storm barriers to protect a site and surrounding infrastructure. These kinds of storms can bring lethal levels of wind and water, both factors that a developer can mitigate against based on a site design but cannot completely eliminate risk.

A final hazard worth mentioning here are wildfires. At the time of this writing, the Western US has experienced a drastic uptick in wildfires with one report showing 5.6 million acres burned, an increase of almost double from last year to date and three times the year before. Climatic factors can be assessed here to understand how arid a region is and then a site analysis could examine the nature of nearby forests to estimate possible threats from wildfires. Projections by state forest agencies can be utilized to calculate these risks.

Endangered Species and Biodiversity

For a real estate development project, the hydrological and hazard conditions on a site are critical to understanding what can be built. An equally pressing, though related question is about existing life on and around a site. Flora and fauna live among wetlands, streams, and lakes, they grow and flourish on steep slopes and contribute to soil quality. These living systems, taken together, can be understood as the biodiversity of a site. The Convention of Biological Diversity defined biodiversity as:

The variability among living organism from all sources including, inter alia, terrestrial, marine, and other aquatic ecosystems and ecological complexes of which they are part: this includes diversity within species, between species, and of ecosystems (Convention of Biologicial Diversity 2006, n.p.)

A properly functioning landscape with high biodiversity can contribute to important ecosystem services as well as human enjoyment (Lindqvist et al. 2016). Healthy ecosystems provide clean air, fresh water, and soils for agriculture, not to mention opportunities for human recreation and general enjoyment of nature (Berry 2007).

Biodiversity is a measure of the health of a landscape and allows us to ask questions like: do particular species dominate more than others, are there key imbalances that threaten broader ecosystems, in what ways are species linked to one another (Hack 2018)? Landscape ecologists study these kinds of questions and conclude that landscapes have three major elements: (1) patches are relatively uniform areas, regarding soil, slopes, and orientation, (2) corridors link these patches, and (3) those spaces between corridors and patches where human activities create great disturbances to a landscape, a matrix (see Figure 6.12) (Hack 2018).

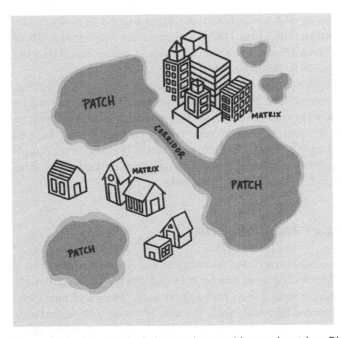

Figure 6.12 Diagram depicting patches, corridors, and matrices. Diagram courtesy of Uma Edulbehram.

To examine biodiversity as part of a site analysis, a first step is a basic mapping of these landscape elements and an exploration of how a proposed new use might disrupt any stable patches or cut off any corridors. Preserving wildlife corridors can go far in enhancing an area's biodiversity, allowing for animals to travel across a site and connect with broader ecological systems in a region. Habitat fragmentation can lead to an imbalance in biodiversity and increase the pressure on endangered species (Sousa-Silva et al. 2014).

National and state laws have been in place since the late twentieth century in many countries. In the United States, the federal Endangered Species Act (16U.S.C § 1538) provides limits on real estate development project on both federal government and private land if there are risks to endangered or threatened species (Thompson 1997; Berry 2007).

Measuring and assessing biodiversity (and the possible presence of endangered species) can go beyond a simple map of landscape elements to involve a cataloging of both plant and animal species – a wildlife inventory (Berry 2007). These types of projects can be quite labor intensive. An abbreviated wildlife inventory involves a limited focus just on keystone species, those that might be particularly critical to an ecosystem or just those species that are easiest to identify and count (Berry 2007).

Much more elaborate analysis can be conducted that explores, scientifically, how rich the species mix is or how healthy the broader ecosystem is for a site (de Baan et al. 2013; Lindner et al. 2014). These advanced methods consider varying scales, including how diverse species are at a single point, in the immediate ecosystem, and in a broader region (Indermuehle et al. 2004). One type of biodiversity assessment tool both quantifies the total number of species, estimates how they are distributed, and then measures how highly correlated each's diversity is with one another (Oliver and Beattie 1996; Cardoso, Rigal, and Carvalho 2015). The most sophisticated tools use DNA from plants or animals to explore biodiversity at the genetic level, introducing extraordinary precision (Smith et al. 2005). Recent innovations have led to using environmental DNA analysis, where scientists study "plant pollen in soil or fish scales in water ... via passive sampling" (Krehenwinkel et al. 2019, p. 3).

An important part of analyzing a site for biodiversity and endangered species is a rough sense of the kinds of mitigation measures that might be likely for a proposed development. In the United States, a common response to a finding of endangered species on a site is for a developer to complete a Habitat Conservation Plan (HCPs) (Langpap and Kerkvliet 2012). An HCP might recommend detailed fieldwork, advanced modeling and analysis, land acquisition, habitat restoration, and ongoing monitoring. These steps are not cheap to implement, with one study concluding that the median cost for project-scale HCPs was almost $5 million and large-scale HCPs was over $100 million (Surrey et al. 2022).

Any proposed new development may impact local and regional biodiversity and endangered species, so a basic accounting of available data and rudimentary mapping of conditions can be critical in informing a site plan. Taking such modest steps can identify costs and challenges early in the real estate development and planning process.

The Site Plan

The ultimate goal of this stage of the real estate development process is the generation of a proposed site plan that reflects not only the myriad of applicable local and state regulations, but also reflects a program that can deliver on the pro forma analysis conducted earlier. Many localities require site plan review as part of their planning process and this document can be a place where developers can negotiate with local authorities.

Architects and landscape architects will be presented later in the book, but can be useful at this early stage by taking the site analysis and converting it into a plan (or help shape a draft site plan that can be used iteratively as part of certain aspects of the site analysis like transportation modeling). Skilled designers and planners can sketch the rough location, size, and shape of structures, infrastructure, and landscaping, attempting to meet minimum requirements of the law but also seeking to meet the requirements of the program. While the program might be simply to build ten duplex housing units, the values of the developer and the community ought to also be explicitly integrated into the program. The exclusion of those values obfuscates that aim of the project and can lead to local resistance.

Developers seeking a smooth, quick, and easy approval process from local authorities will integrate local mission statements from community and master plans into their own program (Frank 2009). One notable example was in the Florida appellate case of *Morgan Co v. Orange County*, in which a developer entered an agreement for immediate rezoning of a property, and requested the city "support and expeditiously process" the request. This case shows that local officials can aid the development process (Fla. Dist. Ct. App. 2002).

Conclusion

With a thoughtful site analysis, a real estate developer can generate a site plan that addresses the minimum requirements of the law while addressing the stated goals of their project – as articulated in a program. These goals need not be limited to the investment parameters enumerated in the pro forma, the goals can be embedded in findings from research presented in this chapter and elsewhere about what it means to create places for people, places that will endure, that will provide benefits and amenities for humankind. This research tells us that creating just, equitable, vibrant, inclusive, and sustainable places can have profound returns and create profits for a real estate developer. The local government development review process, in particular site plan review, provides a forum for local officials to evaluate a project's fit with a community and compliance with local rules. It is also an opportunity to undertake a negotiation to see how best a development proposal can address broader community needs, to create buildings for people.

CASE STUDY: Plaza Roberto Maestas

Project Background

The Plaza Roberto Maestas development in the Beacon Hill neighborhood of Seattle opened in 2016 with 112 rental units, a 12,900-square-foot plaza, the 6,000-square-foot Centilia Cultural Center, 3,200 square feet of retail space, and the expanded José Martí Early Childhood Center (HUD's Office of Policy Development and Research 2018) (see Table 6.1 and Figure 6.13). It was

Table 6.1   Plaza Roberto Maestas Seattle, Washington.

Location	Seattle, WA
Developer(s)	El Centro de la Raza (non-profit)
	Beacon Development Group
Landowner(s)	El Centro de la Raza purchased the property from Seattle Public Schools in the 1990s; light rail 2003 spurred development; eight-year community process
Year Opened	2016
Housing Type	112 rental units
	• 35 one-bedroom
	• 55 two-bedroom
	• 22 three-bedroom apartments
	Between 30% and 60% AMI
People-centered Aspects	Non-luxury housing
	Community-driven amenities (nonprofit space)
	outdoor plaza
	Beacon Hill light-rail station
People-centered Process	Site analysis and planning
Financing	• Development cost $45 million
	• LIHTC: $22.3 million
	• Federal Historic Tax Credit: $1.6 million
	• City of Seattle: $7.9 million

Figure 6.13 Evening view of the Plaza Roberto Maestas. Image courtesy of El Centro de la Raza, Beacon Development Group, William Wright Photography, and SMR Architects.

developed by the non-profit El Centro de la Raza, translated as "The Center for People of All Races" and Beacon Development Group, a non-profit affordable housing firm. El Centro de la Raza purchased the development site in the 1990s from Seattle Public Schools and are headquartered next door to the Plaza Roberto Maestas development (Kroman 2016). A transit-oriented development, Plaza Roberto Maestas is across the street from the Beacon Hill stop on Seattle's light rail. Tile mosaics (see Figures 6.14–6.16) also adorn sections of development with solar panels on the roof.

Site Analysis and Planning

In analyzing and planning for the site, El Centro de la Raza worked with a development consultant Beacon Development Group and identified a number of challenges. For this project, there was no extensive site selection process, El Centro de la Raza had occupied the land as part of a social protest in the 1970s, eventually gaining title to the property. There was a historic school house where they ran their operations and they wanted to use the remainder of the property to build a community center. There is not a lot of funding available to support the construction of a new community center, so instead they came up with the idea of a mixed-use project that would include both the community center (see Figure

Figure 6.14   Tile Mosaics at Plaza Roberto Maestas. Image courtesy of El Centro de la Raza, Beacon Development Group, William Wright Photography, and SMR Architects.

6.17) and subsidized housing (see Figure 6.18). In conducting a site analysis, the development team noted that the site is within the geographic scope of a City of Seattle plan: The North Beacon Hill Neighborhood Plan. The Neighborhood Plan called for new projects to include a mixture of uses, a civic gathering space, and housing near transit, something the project developers heard again in their community engagement ("Jack Kemp Excellence in Affordable and Workforce Housing Awards 2019 Winner: Plaza Roberto Maestas" 2019).

For that kind of mixed-use/public gathering projected use, they examined the constraints and opportunities presented by the property – according to a PowerPoint presentation the developers shared with us (El Centro de la Raza and Beacon Development Group *undated*). First, the site was next to a light rail station and part of the rail line ran under a corner of the property. Public transit is a real

Figure 6.15 Tile Mosaics at Plaza Roberto Maestas. Image courtesy of El Centro de la Raza, Beacon Development Group, William Wright Photography, and SMR Architects.

amenity, but that easement under the property limited excavation on that corner and Seattle city regulations put a maximum on the amount of parking allowed (which in a car-centric city like Seattle represented a challenge). In response, the developer inked a shared use agreement for the parking lot at the old school house so residents in the new building could park there in the evenings and the weekends (El Centro de la Raza and Beacon Development Group *undated*).

That school house was historic and identified early in the site analysis as a potential issue. The developer worked closely with the Washington State Historical Preservation Office and took measures to protect the building as a cultural resource (El Centro de la Raza and Beacon Development Group *undated*).

Another issue that arose in the site analysis was that in order to include child care facilities at the building, state regulations require a minimum open space per child ratio. In this kind of urban setting, that was a problem and the developer

Figure 6.16 Tile Mosaics at Plaza Roberto Maestas. Image courtesy of El Centro de la Raza, Beacon Development Group, William Wright Photography, and SMR Architects.

came up with a creative solution. They got a grant from the City of Seattle Parks' Department to build a city park on their property (see Figure 6.19), which is open to the public all the time, except during the hours that the child care facility is operating (El Centro de la Raza and Beacon Development Group *undated*). This way, the community benefits from a new park, while the developer addresses a site constraint.

Another major finding from the site analysis was that the major road the property has frontage on is designated by the City of Seattle as a "festival" street, which means that it can be shut down to car traffic for fairs. This was recognized as an opportunity and not a challenge: the architects designed a plaza to connect to street to the development so street fairs and festivals could spill out from their project to the street (El Centro de la Raza and Beacon Development Group *undated*).

Figure 6.17 Centilia Cultural Center. Image courtesy of El Centro de la Raza, Beacon Development Group, William Wright Photography, and SMR Architects.

Figure 6.18 Street view of subsidized housing units. Image courtesy of El Centro de la Raza, Beacon Development Group, William Wright Photography, and SMR Architects.

Figure 6.19 Park on project site. Image courtesy of El Centro de la Raza, Beacon Development Group, William Wright Photography, and SMR Architects

The property is adjacent to a neighborhood of single-family homes and the idea of a multi-story mixed use project might have generated not-in-my-backyard (NIMBY) response. Instead, through over 20 public meetings, El Centro de la Raza and Beacon Development Group truly engaged with the community and between the plaza, the park, the childcare facility, and other design ideas, were able to present a project that neighbors were enthusiastic about. At the project's final land use approval meeting at the Seattle City Council, the room was packed and support from the neighbors was unanimous when the developers proposed their project and requested permission to upzone the property from a Neighborhood Business district where maximum heights were 45 feet to a similar district where heights could go up to 60 feet.

People-centered Components

Plaza Roberto Maestas provides 112 rental housing units for low-income families, about half the units are two-bedrooms, with the building restricted to those making between 30% and 60% AMI. When applications for the building first became available six months before move-in, some people lined up over twenty-four hours in advance and over 450 people applied for the units (Kroman 2016). In addition to responding to the need for affordable housing, another people centered component are the amenities. The development includes an expanded childcare center and a cultural center, the development has 3,200 square feet of retail space that has been targeted for small business development and includes a food cart program in the plaza. El Centro de la Raza purchased eight carts and participants have access to a kitchen on site with access to training by the non-profit Ventures, which supports entrepreneurs who have limited support and access to resources and capital (Tu 2017). El Centro de la Raza were intentional in making the plaza an outdoor public space, another people-centered element, for the residents and community. The proximity to the light rail is a further people-centered component of the development.

Case Takeaways

People-centered site analysis and planning processes put the existing neighborhood and community members first, while also being mindful of proximate transportation infrastructure (in this case, a light rail station) and the vast array of other environmental, land use, policy, and other considerations. That forward looking approach resulted in a new development that is welcomed in the community. People-centered components are identified early and potential benefits for existing community members become a part of the development process rather than a rushed, conciliatory addition to gain a permit and begin building.

Note

1 Innumerable considerations will come into play as part of this kind of analysis, but one notable factor in calibrating this kind of model is whether housing on a site is subsidized affordable housing. Currants et al. (2020) found that residents living in affordable housing in urban areas tended to make fewer automobile trips than residents in market-rate housing in suburban areas.

Bibliography

Anon (2017). *History & evolution – El Centro de la Raza*. [online] https://www. elcentrodelaraza.org/history-evolution (accessed November 8, 2022).

Berry, J. (2007). Biodiversity protection. In: *Planning and Urban Design Standards*. (ed. F.R. Steiner and K. Butler). Chicago: APA Press.

Blond, N., Carnevale, C., Douros, J., Finzi, G., Guariso, G., Janssen, S., Maffeis, G. et al. (2017). A framework for integrated assessment modelling. *Air Quality Integrated Assessment: A European Perspective* 9–35.

Bunn, F. and Zannin, P.H.T. (2015). Urban planning-simulation of noise control measures. *Noise Control Engineering Journal* 63 (1): 1–10. doi: 10.3397/1/376301.

Cardoso, P., Rigal, F., and Carvalho, J.C. (2015). BAT – Biodiversity Assessment Tools, an R package for the measurement and estimation of alpha and beta taxon, phylogenetic and functional diversity. *Methods in Ecology and Evolution* 6 (2): 232–236. doi: 10.1111/2041-210x.12310.

Carnevale, C., Finzi, G., Pederzoli, A., Turrini, E., and Volta, M. (2017). Concentration Reduction Apportionment (CRA) Approach: a new methodology to define effective air quality plans. *IFAC-PapersOnLine* 50 (1): 3165–3170.

casetext.com (n.d.). *Morgran Company v. Orange County, 818 So. 2d 640 | Casetext Search + Citator*. [online] https://casetext.com/case/morgran-company-v-orange-county (accessed November 8, 2022).

Cavailhès, J. (2005). Le prix des attributs du logement. *Economie et statistique* 381 (1): 91–123.

Currans, K.M., Abou-Zeid, G., Clifton, K.J. et al. (2020). Improving transportation impact analyses for subsidized affordable housing developments: a data collection and analysis of motorized vehicle and person trip generation. *Cities* 103: 102774. doi: 10.1016/j.cities.2020.102774.

de Baan, L., Alkemade, R., and Koellner, T. (2013). Land use impacts on biodiversity in LCA: a global approach. *The International Journal of Life Cycle Assessment* 18 (6): 1216–1230. doi: 10.1007/s11367-012-0412-0.

Delbosc, A. and Currie, G. (2013). Exploring attitudes of young adults toward cars and driver licensing. *Proceedings of the Australasian Transport Research Forum*, Brisbane, Australia. 2–4.

Fla. Dist. Ct. App. (2002). *Morgan Co v*. Orange County.

Frank, S.P. (2009). Yes in my backyard: developers, government and communities working together through development agreements and community benefit agreements. *Indiana Law Review* [online] 42 (1): 227–256. doi: 10.18060/3988.

Gehl, J. (2010). *Cities for People*. Washington, DC: Island Press.

Hack, G. (2018). *Site Planning: International Practice*. Cambridge: MIT Press.

Hollander, J.B. and Sussman, A. (eds.) (2021). *Urban Experience and Design: International Perspectives on 21st-Century Urban Design and Planning*. London / New York: Routledge.

Hurley, P.J., Physick, W.L., and Luhar, A.K. (2005). TAPM: a practical approach to prognostic meteorological and air pollution modelling. *Environmental Modelling & Software* 20 (6): 737–752.

Indermuehle, N., Oertli, B., Menetrey Perrottet, N., and Sager, L. (2004). *An overview of methods potentially suitable for pond biodiversity assessment. Archives Des Sciences.*

International City/County Management Association. (2000). *The Practice of Local Government Planning.* Chicago: American Planning Association.

Krehenwinkel, H., Pomerantz, A., and Prost, S. (2019). Genetic biomonitoring and biodiversity assessment using portable sequencing technologies: current uses and future directions. *Genes* 10 (11): 858. doi: 10.3390/genes10110858.

Kroman, D. (2016). *Hundreds vie for a chance at affordable housing | Crosscut.* [online] crosscut.com. https://crosscut.com/2016/02/housing-chances-draw-a-crowd-with-many-sure-to-lose-out (accessed November 8, 2022).

Langpap, C. and Kerkvliet, J. (2012). Endangered species conservation on private land: assessing the effectiveness of habitat conservation plans. *Journal of Environmental Economics and Management* 64 (1): 1–15. doi: 10.1016/j.jeem.2012.02.002.

Le Boennec, R. and Salladarré, F. (2017). The impact of air pollution and noise on the real estate market. The case of the 2013 European Green Capital: Nantes, France. *Ecological Economics* 138: 82–89.

Lee, S.-W., Chang, S.I., and Park, Y.-M. (2008). Utilizing noise mapping for environmental impact assessment in a downtown redevelopment area of Seoul, Korea. *Applied Acoustics* 69 (8): 704–714. doi: 10.1016/j.apacoust.2007.02.009.

Lindner, J., Bos, U., Niblick, B. et al. (2014). Proposal of a unified biodiversity impact assessment method. *Proceedings of the 9th International Conference on Life Cycle Assessment in the Agri-Food Sector (LCA Food 2014)*, San Francisco, CA, USA, October 8–10, 2014.

Lindqvist, M., Palme, U., and Lindner, J.P. (2016). A comparison of two different biodiversity assessment methods in LCA—a case study of Swedish spruce forest. *The International Journal of Life Cycle Assessment* 21 (2): 190–201. doi: 10.1007/s11367-015-1012-6.

Liu, C.Y. and Painter, G. (2012). Travel behavior among Latino immigrants. *Journal of Planning Education and Research* 32 (1): 62–80. doi: 10.1177/0739456x11422070.

McDonald, N.C. (2015). Are millennials really the 'go-nowhere' generation? *Journal of Planning Education and Research* [online] 81 (2): 90–103. doi: 10.1080/01944363.2015.1057196.

Moreno-Mateos, D. and Comin, F.A. (2010). Integrating objectives and scales for planning and implementing wetland restoration and creation in agricultural landscapes. *Journal of Environmental Management* 91 (11): 2087–2095. doi: 10.1016/j.jenvman.2010.06.002.

Oliver, I. and Beattie, A.J. (1996). Designing a cost-effective invertebrate survey: a test of methods for rapid assessment of biodiversity. *Ecological Applications* 6 (2): 594–607. doi: 10.2307/2269394.

Seattle, Washington: mixed-use development provides affordable housing at Plaza Roberto Maestas. (2018). [online] *HUD's Office of Policy Development and Research.* https://www.huduser.gov/portal/casestudies/study-022018.html.

Smith, M.A., Fisher, B.L., and Hebert, P.D.N. (2005). DNA barcoding for effective biodiversity assessment of a hyperdiverse arthropod group: the ants of Madagascar. *Philosophical Transactions of the Royal Society B: Biological Sciences* 360 (1462): 1825–1834. doi: 10.1098/rstb.2005.1714.

Sousa-Silva, R., Alves, P., Honrado, J., and Lomba, A. (2014). Improving the assessment and reporting on rare and endangered species through species distribution models. *Global Ecology and Conservation* 2: 226–237. doi: 10.1016/j.gecco.2014.09.011.

Steiner, F.R. and Butler, K. (2007). *Planning and Urban Design Standards.* Chicago: APA Press.

Surrey, K.C., Iacona, G., Madsen, B. et al. (2022). Habitat Conservation Plans provide limited insight into the cost of complying with the Endangered Species Act. *Conservation Science and Practice* 4 (6). doi: 10.1111/csp2.12673.

Sussman, A. and Hollander, J.B.. (2021). *Cognitive Architecture: Designing for How We Respond to the Built Environment,* 2e. London / New York: Routledge.

Thompson, B.H. (1997). The endangered species act: a case study in takings & incentives. *Stanford Law Review* 49 (2): 305. doi: 10.2307/1229299.

Tu, J. (2017). *Food-cart initiative puts Latino entrepreneurs on a path to their dreams.* [online] *The Seattle Times.* https://www.seattletimes.com/business/retail/food-carts-put-latino-entrepreneurs-on-a-path-to-their-dreams.

ULI Americas (2019). *Jack Kemp excellence in affordable and workforce housing awards 2019 winner: Plaza Roberto Maestas.* [online] https://americas.uli.org/jack-kemp-excellence-in-affordable-and-workforce-housing-awards-2019-prm (accessed November 8, 2022).

Unit (2006). *Article 2: use of terms.* [online] *Convention of Biological Diversity.* https://www.cbd.int/convention/articles/?a=cbd-02.

U.S. Geological Survey's Water Science School (2018). *Freshwater (Lakes and Rivers) and the Water Cycle.* June 8. https://www.usgs.gov/special-topics/water-science-school/science/freshwater-lakes-and-rivers-and-water-cycle (accessed October 1, 2022).

Xu, B., Luo, L., and Lin, B. (2016). A dynamic analysis of air pollution emissions in China: evidence from nonparametric additive regression models. *Ecological Indicators* 63: 346–358.

Yuen, F. (2014). A vision of the environmental and occupational noise pollution in Malaysia. *Noise and Health* 16 (73): 427. doi: 10.4103/1463-1741.144429.

7

Architecture and Landscape Architecture

Architects and landscape architects may play a role in shaping the site plan discussed in Chapter 5, otherwise they are introduced slightly later to design the detailed plans for buildings and landscaping. These plans, also known as blueprints, serve as an instructional manual for the construction team to actually do the building – a step we will explore in detail in Chapter 9. In this chapter, the specific role of these architects and landscape architects is examined, the work that they do, and how they can contribute to people-centric real estate development.

A little context is first helpful. Architects and landscape architects are licensed professionals, which means that states require certain educational background, continuing education, and the passing of a standardized examination. These high standards exist for good reason, if architects make serious errors, buildings can collapse, and people can die. The hazards that come from unprepared landscape architects have more to do with the threat of flooding without properly drained land, which can also cause serious damage and injury. Strategic landscape design can alleviate the impacts of such natural disasters. The players introduced so far in the real estate development process have been accountants, financial analysts, appraisers, bankers, and site planners. Professionals in these two design fields, are more intimately involved in bringing their professional judgment and expertise to bear on the physical form of a real estate development project – dangers, risks, and all.

When these designers begin on a real estate development project it is usually under contract from a real estate developer, but some development companies have in-house designers. No matter how they come on board, designers bring with them a mix of practical experience and their education. Both architects and landscape architects come from a long tradition of apprenticeship, where after formal education they work directly under a licensed professional for a number of

Buildings for People: Responsible Real Estate Development and Planning, First Edition.
Justin B. Hollander and Nicole E. Stephens.
© 2023 John Wiley & Sons, Inc. Published 2023 by John Wiley & Sons, Inc.

years before being able to practice independently. In this way, accumulated knowledge is passed down from generation to generation, not just at the university but in the firms.

This apprenticeship tradition was quite effective for millennia at conveying classical ideas around proportionality, hierarchy, use of materials, form, bulk, ornamentation, and density (Buras 2020). The Pantheon (125 CE), Colosseum (80 CE), and the Temple of Olympian Zeus (131 CE), ancient buildings that still stand today and are widely celebrated as welcoming, inviting, and human-friendly (see Figures 7.1–7.3). From the time of Ancient Greece, architects had an uncanny sense of what was needed to create buildings for people, a tradition that was briefly lost but resurrected by Renaissance writers like Giacomo Barozzi da Vignola in his *The Five Orders of Architecture* (1562), Andrea Palladio and *The Four Books of Architecture* (1570), and Leon Battista Alberti with his *De re aedificatoria* (1452). Neo-classical design exploded in this period with particularly monumental buildings including St. Peter's Basilica (1506) and Villa Farnesina (1509) in Rome (see Figures 7.4 and 7.5), classical principles continued to shape vernacular (otherwise known as ordinary) design for centuries. The important architectural works of the seventeenth, eighteenth, and nineteenth centuries drew on classicism, while also responding to historic building traditions that went back to humans' earliest shelters.

In response to local conditions and not necessarily with the expertise of trained architects, people have been building to meet their needs for shelter since humans

Figure 7.1   Front view of the Pantheon in Rome, Italy. Nono vlf / Wikimedia Commons / CC BY-SA 4.0.

Figure 7.2 Colosseum amphitheater in Rome, Italy. Ank Kumar / Wikimedia Commons / CC BY-SA 4.0.

Figure 7.3 Temple of the Olympian Zeus. Jean-Pierre Dalbéra / Wikimedia Commons / CC BY 2.0.

first roamed the savannas of Africa a couple hundred thousand years ago (Sussman and Hollander 2021). These building have always relied on local materials, because that was what was available. That meant wood in America, marble in Europe, white stone in the Middle East, bamboo in East Asia, and straw thatch

Figure 7.4 St. Peter's Basilica from Saint Peter's Square in Vatican City. Mstyslav Chernov / Wikimedia Commons / CC BY-SA 3.0.

Figure 7.5 Villa Farnesina in Italy. Peter1936F / Wikimedia Commons / CC BY-SA 3.0.

roofs in Africa. What is quite remarkable about these traditional building styles is that despite their variation in materials and construction techniques and their responses to different climates, they share many of the same design characteristics (see Figures 7.6 and 7.7). They are bilaterally symmetrical, they employ a rigid hierarchy of top-middle-bottom, and their elements are primarily vertically

Figure 7.6 Traditional *Honai* house architecture in the village of Obia, Papau New Guinea. Irfantraveller / Wikimedia Commons / CC BY-SA 4.0.

Figure 7.7 Ancient stone cottage with tiled roof. Minakryn Ruslan / Adobe Stock.

oriented. This ancient building style meshed with the classical impulses described earlier in the centuries to follow the Renaissance, with the building of the Schauspielhaus (1819), the Bibliotheque Sainte Genevieve (1840), and the Stieglitz Museum of Applied Arts (1896) (see Figures 7.8–7.10 here) which were each influenced by historical styles (Neville 2020).

Figure 7.8 Schauspielhaus in Berlin, Germany. Ansgar Koreng / Wkimedia Commons / CC BY 3.0 de.

Figure 7.9 Interior reading room of the Biblioteque Saint-Genevieve in Paris, France. Marie-Lan Nguyen / Wkimedia Commons / CC BY 2.0 fr.

But then something changed in the beginning of the twentieth century. It was the birth of modernism. Not just impacting architecture, but re-arranging broad societal tastes and sensibilities, modernism meant a detachment from the past, an embrace of machines and new technology, a different order based on science and rationality (Scott 2008; Walz 2013). For architecture, modernism took flight at the Bauhaus School in Germany (MacCarthy 2019). These

Figure 7.10 Main entrance of Stieglitz Museum of Applied Arts in St. Petersburg, Russia. Alex 'Florstein' Fedorov / Wkimedia Commons / CC BY-SA 4.0.

Bauhaus designers eschewed traditional design and spoke of the power of building new materials and technologies to create heretofore impossible building forms (Chen and He 2013). (See Figures 7.11 and 7.12). This can be seen in buildings including Le Corbusier's Villa Savoye, and the Seagram building and Barcelona Pavilion both by Mies Van der Rohe (see Figures 7.13 and 7.14).

The Bauhaus founder, Walter Gropius, left Europe and began teaching at the Graduate School of Design at Harvard University in 1937, creating what would soon become the North American headquarters for modern architecture (Alofsin 2002; MacCarthy 2019). Along with Swiss architect Le Corbusier and German-born Mies Van De Rohe, these founding fathers of modern architecture led a global revolution in the design professions that transformed buildings, landscapes, and public spaces. It is worth mentioning that acolytes of these modernist leaders followed in both the landscape architecture as well as the urban design and planning fields, including particularly prolific designers like Marcel Breuer and IM Pei (Pearlman 2007).

Histories of architecture seldom interrogate this drastic turn in the design professions, from the truly human approaches in vernacular and classical design to

Figure 7.11 Bauhaus-Building Dessau design headquarters designed by Walter Gropius. Alex Spyrosdrakopoulos / Wkimedia Commons / CC BY-SA 4.0.

Figure 7.12 Instance of Bauhau building design. Tegula / Pixabay.

Figure 7.13   Le Corbusier's Villa Sovoye in Poissy, France. SoiHong / Wkimedia Commons / CC BY-SA 4.0.

Figure 7.14   Exterior view of Barcelona Pavilion by Mies Van De Rohe. Mcginnly / Wkimedia Commons / CC BY-SA 3.0.

the truly inhuman modernist approach. At perhaps the zenith of modern architecture popularity globally, two titans clashed in a public forum at the Harvard Design School in 1982. Christopher Alexander, renowned traditional/ classical architect and author of the seminal *A Pattern Language* (1977) debated the widely celebrated modernist designer, Peter Eisenman. The event was titled "Contrasting Concepts of Harmony in Architecture" and went to the very core of the discipline: what was the purpose of architecture? Alexander offered his answer plainly: the purpose of architecture is to encourage and support life-giving activity, dreams, and playfulness. Eisenman's response was a defense of modernity: "architecture as a conceptual, cultural, and intellectual enterprise" (*Architectural Review* 2013). He went on to recount the story of how his young children were terrified of nuclear war and how critically important it was for new buildings to speak to that angst and stress, as his designs do so well (see Figures 7.15–7.19). Alexander's response was that to build such structures was simply

Figure 7.15 Christopher Alexander's Higashino High school campus project in Tokyo, Japan. Peter Morville / Flickr.

cruel to children and adults, alike. Alexander insisted that architects have a responsibility to shape human settlements in a way that puts people at ease, helps them to relax, and brings them joy.

In the years since the Alexander-Eisenman debate, modernism has lost its luster and a New Urbanism has risen. An architectural style emerging from the ashes of classical and traditional design, leading practitioners and writers including Andres Duany, Elizabeth Plater-Zybek (2003), Peter Katz (1994), and Peter Calthorpe (1995) built buildings and entire communities that rejected modernism and added back in ornamentation, bilateral symmetry, hierarchy, and the use of local building materials (see Figure 7.20). These designs focused on the human experience in a way that modernism seemed to prefer the automobile with regard to scale. With front porches, small yards, and sidewalks to connect to other homes, this style gained popularity fast and began to garner global attention as an emerging style (Calthorpe 1995).

Figure 7.16 The Sala House in Albany, California designed by Christopher Alexander. Ekyono / Wkimedia Commons / CC BY-SA 4.0.

Figure 7.17 Wider view of the Sala House in Albany, California. Ekyono / Wkimedia Commons / CC BY-SA 4.0.

Figure 7.18 Peter Eisenman's City of Culture of Galicia, a complex of libraries and other cultural buildings in Santiago de Compostela, Spain. Luis Miguel Bugallo Sánchez / Wkimedia Commons / CC BY-SA 3.0.

Figure 7.19 Checkpoint Charlie Museum in Berlin, Germany designed by Peter Eisenman. Arbalete / Wkimedia Commons / Public Domain.

Figure 7.20 Seaside, Florida a community exemplative of new-urbanism designed Andres Duany and Elizabeth Plater-Zybek. Steve Tiesdell Legacy Collection / Flickr / CC BY 2.0.

Cognitive Architecture

This speedy overview of the history of architecture was intended to help you understand the role that style plays in shaping building design. What was missing from the above was a deeper probing of why certain design characteristics have persisted since antiquity, the answer lies in the human mind.

For billions of years, the gears of evolution have been turning in creatures as small as paramecium and as large as Blue Whales, as generations pass on, they conserve those genetic features that give them an advantage at surviving. Likewise, us humans have benefited from evolution with regard to how we take in the world around us. We are primarily a visual species, so we observe what is around us through our eyes – estimates are that as much as 90% of the information that flows into our brains comes from our eyes (Mlodinow 2013). Our other senses pick up still more crucial data, hearing, touch, taste, and smell. But those visual cues are what are largely telling us when to fight and when to flee, when to be hyper aware and when to relax.

A growing body of science and research has demonstrated that the form, bulk, and arrangement of architecture, landscape, and urban design can have a measurable effect on humans' well-being and stress levels, what attracts us to a place, what we remember, and what repels us (Sussman and Hollander 2021; Goldhagen 2019; Hollander and Sussman 2021). What architectural historians used to simply report on as a shift in style from one period to another can now be reframed in biological terms: there are certain designs that put people at ease, as Christopher Alexander wrote and spoke about, and there are others that make people stressed and seek to avoid, like the work of Peter Eisenman and many modern architects (Hollander and Sussman 2021). This science can be organized into five major themes, from the Sussman and Hollander (2021) book *Cognitive Architecture: Designing for How We Respond to the Built Environment*:

Edges Matter: This principle describes how as pedestrians we are a "wall-hugging" species. The more designers are aware of thigmotaxis as a billion-year-old biological trait, the better they will understand why well-defined corridor streets encourage our walking and the imperative of creating them in suburban and urban places;

Patterns Matter: This principle reminds us that the human mind prioritizes vision. We evolved in a world of visual complexity and relish visual stimulation, not sameness nor blankness. We are also biologically designed to process, emotionally engage with, and remember facial patterns over other forms. The template for the face is in us before birth;

Shapes Carry Weight: This principle recognizes that humans are programmed to prefer certain forms over others; we carry innate biological biases toward bilateral symmetric shapes, and for curved versus straight, or jagged lines or forms;

Storytelling Is Key: This principle most identifies us as human; our narrative capacity, a consequence of our species' unique neural circuitry, helps us engage with others, with places, with a shared past and enables the creation of identity. Most popular designed places engage this aspect of human uniqueness in some manner.

Nature Is Our Context: emphasizes the importance of biophilic elements in our designs, both inside and out. An artifact of evolution, we always require connection to the fabric that made us.

What do Architects do

This chapter thus far has provided a valuable overview of the history of design and how recent scientific advances reframe the role of architects and their purpose. With this knowledge in hand, it does seem that Christopher Alexander won that debate from Harvard back in 1982. The architect has an important role to play in fitting the assigned program on the developer selected site, but with this Cognitive Architecture perspective, they can also use their design skills to create places that people will feel welcome, invited, comfortable, where they can enjoy life.

In addition, the architect must also be sure their design complies with all applicable local building codes, state, and national laws – in particular around accessibility and environmental performance. Architects are gifted at understanding spatial relationships and can provide unparalleled service to a real estate developer in resolving conflicts between the assigned program, site conditions, and other legal or policy constraints. Through a studio design process, architects work in small teams to explore, debate, sketch, and re-sketch a range of such solutions. This iterative process can take time and inspiration doesn't always come promptly, but a poor design solution will not benefit a developer.

A particularly noteworthy dimension to landscape architects' work today is their role in the reuse and redevelopment of brownfields (Hollander, Kirkwood, Gold 2010). When a property is impaired due to environmental contamination (as introduced in Chapter 5), landscape design decisions can be a big part of the development solution. Landscape architects have expertise in the kinds of plants that can help extract contamination from polluted soil and clear impacted groundwater (Kennen and Kirkwood 2015). Carefully selected plantings can play a key role in the reuse of these brownfields and can complement more expensive solutions that environmental engineers may need to introduce (like long-term pumping, construction of barriers, and large-scale soil excavation).

Once the architect has a design that they and their developer client are comfortable with, it is again time to re-engage with local (and sometimes state) authorities through an extended site plan (see Figure 7.21) or design review process. Most local authorities who have any meaningful discretion in the project review process will expect highly detailed drawings and illustrations before giving a final approval. Thus, the architect will need to be a part of the real estate developer's team in presenting the project to approving officials, the exception only being for

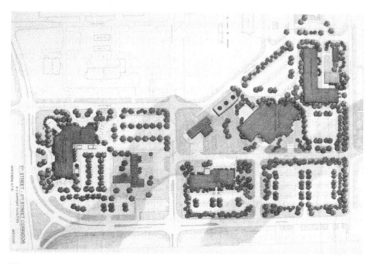

Figure 7.21 Architect's site plan drawing of aircraft support facilities at Whiteman Air Force Base in Missouri, United States.

by-right projects. In larger municipalities, architects may work in-house for the government body, alongside urban planners, to analyze a proposed project and offer feedback to a real estate developer.

The end result of such approvals allows the architect to go beyond the design solution and preliminary renderings of a project to the final deliverable: construction drawings. This last step of the architect's design process takes the rough proportionalities, approximate square footage, estimated materials, and finalizes each of these in formal blueprint documents that are then submitted to a construction team (to be discussed in Chapter 9). During the construction process, architects will maintain an oversight role to ensure their designs are being executed correctly and to respond to unforeseen modifications in the project, like a change in the availability in certain building material or unexpected environmental contamination on a property.

What Do Landscape Architects Do

The landscape architecture field was similarly impacted by the rise of modernism and likewise benefits from today's Cognitive Architecture perspective, helping to guide landscape architects toward shaping outdoor places in a way that supports mental health and well-being. Some of the principles described above demand particular attention from landscape architects, like the need to create well-defined edges and to reinforce our innate connection with nature. The purpose of landscape architecture becomes then to shape outdoor spaces through the use of plants, paths, changes in topography, and other environmental design in the service of creating places that attract people and help them feel comfortable.

In most real estate development projects, landscape architects work either directly for architects or in a support role to them. While the landscape architect may play an outsized role in shaping the early site plan for a development, the real financial generating possibility of most real estate developments lie in the buildings and hence architects' roles are pre-eminent. No building will attract high rents or sell at a good price without decent landscaping; the reverse is not true: a beautifully designed landscape is insufficient to generate a good return for investors – they need a building (the one possible exception might be the development of golf courses which are led by landscape architects).

Landscape decisions, like an architect's, are constrained by local and state rules on plantings, shrubbery, and lawns. A landscape architect needs to solve a different flavor of design solution, addressing the requirements of their program (flower gardens, two rows of hedges, impervious parking lot for five cars), while attending to the human needs outlined in the Cognitive Architecture principles. The landscape architect generally works closely with the architect in a similar (or even the same) studio environment, going through multitudes of various design solutions until reaching one that meets all requirements (see examples in Figures 7.22 and 7.23). Often in tandem with the architect, the landscape architect then shares these landscape plans with the developer and is a likely participant in any site plan or design review process through the local government (as with architects, some landscape architects work directly for local governments, helping to review proposals before them).

Figure 7.22 Instance of landscape architecture at Rose Kennedy Greenway in Boston's North End. cowee10 / Pixabay.

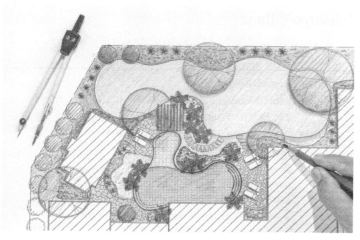

Figure 7.23 Example of landscape architect design for a villa backyard. toa555 / Adobe Stock.

After receiving government approval, the landscape architect finalizes their plans in similar blueprint construction documents that give detailed guidance to a landscaper to implement the design. Just like an architect will continue to play a role in overseeing the implementation of their design, landscape architects tend to be a presence on site ensuring that the landscape contractor is following their blueprint successfully and responding to unforeseen changes.

Conclusion

Architects and landscape architects come from a long tradition of providing specialized expertise in the real estate development and planning process. Their knowledge of buildings and landscapes can be core to a developer's plans and for communicating those plans to government review agencies. A checkered history was presented earlier of how design theory was hijacked by modernism and since then places have been built across the planet that eschew fundamental scientific understanding of human beings. Hope rests in a newly embraced framework for designing the built environment grounded instead in the latest psychology, neuroscience, and evolutionary biology research. There is a critical role for architects and landscape architects to play in adopting this approach, but just as important is the urban designer who shapes the spaces between buildings, the public realm, and the broad human experience of a place. What follows is a case study of Arroyo Village, including a review of the role that architecture and landscape architecture played. The next chapter introduces the urban designer and planner and reviews their role in real estate development and planning.

CASE STUDY: Arroyo Village

Table 7.1 Arroyo Village Denver, Colorado.

Location	Denver, Colorado
Developer(s)	Rocky Mountain Communities (RMC) (non-profit)
	The Delores Project (non-profit)
Landowner(s)	Rocky Mountain Communities (RMC)
Year Opened	July 2019
Housing Type	60-bed homeless shelter for women and transgender individuals
	130 housing units
	• 35 one-bedroom apartment units of permanent supportive housing (0–30% AMI)
	• 95 1, 2, and 3-bedroom affordable housing units (50% AMI)

Table 7.1 (Continued)

People-centered Aspects	Non-luxury housing
	Community amenity: homeless shelter
	Transit-oriented development
People-centered Process	Landscape architecture and architecture
Financing	• $13.2 million in equity from federal low-income housing tax credits (LIHTCs)
	• $4.2 million in equity from Colorado state LIHTCs
	• Freddie Mac issued the project a $10.6 million permanent tax-exempt loan
	• The Colorado Housing Investment Fund loaned the project $3 million
	• The city and county of Denver contributed a $1.3 million forgivable loan
	• The state's HOME Investment Partnerships Program awarded a $1 million grant

Project Background

Arroyo Village (see Figures 7.24 and 7.25) in Denver was a $38 million development spearheaded by two non-profits: Rocky Mountain Communities (RMC), an affordable housing provider and the Delores Project, a shelter provider (HUD's Office of Policy Development and Research 2021) (see Table 7.1). Both providers operated

Figure 7.24 Bird's eye view of Arroyo Village. Courtesy of Shopworks.

Figure 7.25   Street view of Arroyo Village. Courtesy of Shopworks.

separate facilities on adjacent parcels prior to their collaboration and combination of the site. During the construction period, care was taken to continue to provide shelter services and interim housing for those displaced while new apartments were built. The local utility provider, Xcel Energy, awarded Arroyo Village more than $68,000 in incentives for environmentally sustainable building components, such as the use of energy-saving appliances like low-flow fixtures and water-saving appliances, the installation of high-efficiency windows and increased roof and walls insulation (which saves energy when heating and cooling the structure) and site improvements that would enable future solar panels (HUD's Office of Policy Development and Research 2021).

Landscape and Architecture

Aesthetics can be the first thing that a developer might cut back on if they are trying to save money. In a people-centered process though, landscape and architectural pieces are not sacrificed and are instead seen as a tool to help the development and the people living there succeed. Arroyo Village utilizes trauma-informed design (TID):

> TID centers on the belief that spaces should be designed for healing, especially as it relates to mental health, meaning a focus on the following values: dignity, hope, and self-esteem; empowerment and personal control;

safety, security, and privacy; peace of mind; community and connection; and joy, beauty, and meaning

> *("Jack Kemp Excellence in Affordable and Workforce Housing Awards 2020 Winner: Arroyo Village" 2020).*

Shopworks Architecture was the architecture and design team and identified six core values of their TID approach: **(1) Hope, Dignity, and Self-Esteem, (2) Connection and Community, (3) Joy, Beauty, and Meaning, (4) Peace of Mind, (5) Empowerment and Personal Control**, and **(6) Safety, Security, and Privacy** (Shopworks Architecture et al. 2021 p. 7). This was further distilled into three concepts called, "The 3 C's of Designing for Health and Healing: Choice, Community, and Comfort" (ibid p. 9). Some examples of this at Arroyo include the stairwells that had substantial lighting, cut-out windows, and longer corridors (Winfield 2021). The project rejected the utilitarian ideology of modernism to focus on the mental health and well-being of the buildings' occupants and visitors, leaning into a Cognitive Architecture perspective.

Landscaping at the property was not some kind of afterthought, but rather fit directly with their TID approach: the project features outdoor space that functions as a sensory healing garden, along with space for residents to grow their own gardens (see Figures 7.26 and 7.27). The landscaping and building design elements change the narrative for residents, shaking any institutional feeling. In a local article about the project, one resident was interviewed and was quoted as saying "I don't feel like I'm in a shelter. I feel like I'm home" (Singer 2020).

Welcoming design elements, artwork, color, and biophilic elements are people-centered details that were incorporated throughout the building's landscape and architecture.

People-centered Components

People-centered components at Arroyo include affordable housing, a community driven amenity, and access to public transportation. While not a part of the development, it is notable that Arroyo is also adjacent to a large city park. Upon completion, Arroyo Village included 35 supportive housing units for formerly homeless individuals, 95 workforce housing units at 50% area median income (AMI), and a 60-bed shelter for women and transgender individuals in the community, the partnership between the non-profits enabled a continuum of services all on one site ("Jack Kemp Excellence in Affordable and Workforce Housing Awards 2020 Winner: Arroyo Village" 2020). Arroyo is a transit-oriented development adjacent to Denver's light-rail (see Figure 7.28) and across the street from the newly redone Paco Sánchez Park. The park is a 30-acre green space that includes a skate park and a music-themed playground

Figure 7.26 Outdoor area at Arroyo village includes space for gardening. Courtesy of Shopworks.

Figure 7.27 Outdoor area at Arroyo village includes space for gathering. Courtesy of Shopworks.

Figure 7.28 Station at Arroyo Village. Courtesy of Shopworks.

with activity pods that honor the founder of Denver's first Spanish-language radio station (Pintos 2020).

Case Takeaways

While a sentiment exists that a simple roof is enough, there is opportunity for so much more both for the people being housed and the community. Housing is home and providing housing for people who are struggling and/or have struggled can be transformational. People-centered components and processes honor that. Incorporating people-centered landscape and architecture concepts like trauma-informed design only provide greater care and comfort to people living there, helping them to succeed. Co-locating housing and services for this at-risk population elevates the social impact of real estate development.

Bibliography

Alofsin, A. (2002). *The Struggle for Modernism: Architecture, Landscape Architecture, and City Planning at Harvard*. New York: WW Norton & Company.

Artemel, A.J.P. (2013). *Peter versus Peter: Eisenman And Zumthor's theoretical throwdown*. http://architizer.com/blog/peter-versus-peter (accessed July 2, 2022).

Buras, N.H. (2020). *The Art of Classic Planning: Building Beautiful and Enduring Communities*. Cambridge: Harvard University Press.

Calthorpe, P. (1995). *The Next American Metropolis: Ecology, Community, and the American Dream*. New York: Princeton Architectural Press.

Chen, W. and He, Z. (2013). The analysis of the influence and inspiration of the Bauhaus on contemporary design and education. *Engineering* 5 (4): 323–328. doi: 10.4236/eng.2013.54044.

Duany, A., Plater-Zyberk, E., and Alminana, R. (2003). *The New Civic Art: Elements of Town Planning*. Rizzoli.

Goldhagen, S.W. (2019). *WELCOME TO YOUR WORLD: How the Built Environment Shapes Our Lives*. New York: HarperCollins.

Hollander, J.B., Kirkwood, N., and Gold, J. (2010). *Principles of Brownfields Regeneration: Clean-up, Design, and Re-use of Derelict Land*. Washington, DC: Island Press.

Hollander, J.B. and Sussman, A. (2021). *Urban experience and design: International perspectives on 21st-century urban design and planning*. London / New York: Routledge.

HUD's Office of Policy Development and Research (2021). Arroyo Village Provides a Full Spectrum of Housing in a Transit-Oriented Development Denver, Colorado. *PD&R Edge*. https://www.huduser.gov/portal/pdredge/pdr-edge-inpractice-110921. html (accessed July 2, 2022).

Jack Kemp Excellence in Affordable and Workforce Housing Awards 2020 Winner: Arroyo Village. 2020. Urban Land Institute: Americas. August 10, 2020. https:// americas.uli.org/jack-kemp-excellence-in-affordable-and-workforce-housing-awards-2020-arroyo-village/.

Katz, P. (1994). *The New Urbanism: Toward an Architecture of Community*. New York, NY: McGraw-Hill.

Kennen, K. and Kirkwood, N. (2015). *Phyto: Principles and Resources for Site Remediation and Landscape Design*. New York/London: Routledge.

MacCarthy, F. (2019). *Gropius: The Man Who Built the Bauhaus*. Cambridge and Massachusetts: The Belknap Press of Harvard University Press.

Markowsky, G. (2017). Information theory. In: *Encyclopedia Britannica*. (accessed August 28, 2019).

Mlodinow, L. (2013). *Subliminal: How Your Unconscious Mind Rules Your Behavior*. New York: Vintage.

Neville, K. (2020). The theory and practice of eclecticism in Eighteenth-Century European Architecture. *Journal of the Society of Architectural Historians* 79 (2): 152–170.

Pearlman, J.E. (2007). *Inventing American Modernism: Joseph Hudnut, Walter Gropius, and the Bauhaus Legacy at Harvard*. Charlottesville: University of Virginia Press.

Pintos, P. (2020). *Paco Sanchez Park / Dig Studio*. ArchDaily. December 10, 2020. https://www.archdaily.com/952878/paco-sanchez-park-dig-studio.

Scott, J.C. (2008). *Seeing Like a State: How Certain Schemes to Improve the Human Condition Have Failed*. New Haven CT: Yale University Press.

Shopworks Architecture, University of Denver Center for Housing and Homelessness Research, and Group14 Engineering (2021). *Trauma Informed Design Process.* https://shopworksarc.com/wp-content/uploads/2021/10/TID_Process_10_12_2021.pdf.

Singer, D. (2020). *Using trauma-informed design, buildings become tools for recovery.* [online] Collective Colorado. https://collective.coloradotrust.org/stories/using-trauma-informed-design-buildings-become-tools-for-recovery (accessed October 15, 2022).

Special issue on Architecture and Representation. (2013). In: *Architecture, syntax, and the emergence of a new subjectivity: Iman Ansari in conversation with Peter Eisenman.* Architectural Review.

Sussman, A. and Hollander, J.B. (2021). *Cognitive architecture: Designing for how we respond to the built environment,* 2e. London / New York: Routledge.

Walz, R. (2013). *Modernism.* New York/London: Routledge.

Winfield, Carl. (2021). *What Is Trauma-Informed Design?* Next City, October 20, 2021. https://nextcity.org/urbanist-news/what-is-trauma-informed-design.

8

Urban Design and Planning

The layout and spacing of building, the arrangement of landscape elements, the crafting of the public realm, these are the jobs of the urban designer. By virtue of mentioning the words "building" and "landscape," it should be abundantly clear that an urban designer cannot work in isolation, but as part of a team of architects and landscape architects. In fact, the urban designer serves also as a real estate development team's conduit to in-house urban planners or planners working at government review offices. The urban designer speaks the same language as the urban planner, with skill sets closer to architecture than public policy. On a continuum from design focused to policy focused, architects and landscape architects are all the way on the design side, planners all the way on the policy side, and urban designers in the middle (see Figure 8.1).

It is worth discussing education a bit here because it sheds some light on how this continuum is actually operationalized. While most real estate firms are staffed by professionals trained in business, including finance, accounting, and marketing, the professional services teams described in Chapter 7 and this chapter have very different educational backgrounds. All the way on the design side of the continuum, the architects and landscape architects learn how to think spatially; they spend their waking hours in a design studio (briefly described in the previous chapter) pouring over geometries, alignments, scale, and bulk to solve design problems. Informed by some theory and history, these designers use trial and error to try new ideas, test them, learn from them, and then try something new. Failure is their fuel.

In addition, they receive advanced training in construction materials, physics, engineering, climate, and botany, so they know what is needed to design buildings and landscapes. On the policy side of the continuum sit urban planners, whose education tends to be grounded in the social sciences, where they study

Buildings for People: Responsible Real Estate Development and Planning, First Edition.
Justin B. Hollander and Nicole E. Stephens.
© 2023 John Wiley & Sons, Inc. Published 2023 by John Wiley & Sons, Inc.

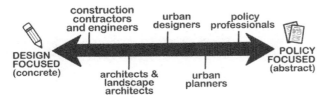

Figure 8.1 Design to policy continuum. Diagram courtesy of Uma Edulbehram.

economics, demography, political science, environmental science, law, philosophy, and geography. A planner learns how to measure the economic or environmental impact of a proposed new development, how well it comports with local, state, and federal laws, and whether it serves a public need in the community. Planners also have an understanding of transportation, with deep knowledge of the various modes of transport (walking, biking, transit, driving) and the strengths and weaknesses of each. Through multi-year projections around changes in a community, a focus on the future priorities or challenges in a place, the planner thinks big and long-term.

Half-way between this broad-scale, policy attention of the planner and the very near term, site-specific focus of the architect or landscape architect, we find the urban designer. With training in both the policy elements that a planner studies and the design elements an architect studies, the urban designer seeks to build bridges between the two sides by shaping site-level designs to think bigger, and reining in big plans to make them practical at the site level.

Urban designers often work as part of a real estate development team, helping to shape the siting and layout of buildings and landscape elements, as well as a liaison with local government officials. They can also be found on the staffs of those local governments, working alongside urban planners to assist in the review of proposed real estate development projects. Less focused on the legal, policy, or economic portions of a proposed development (that an urban planner might have more expertise in), the urban designer would offer more direct critiques around the treatment of the public realm, how buildings are sited, or how streetscapes might be impacted.

The urban planner helps to write zoning and other development regulations so they are a key partner for the real estate developer in interpreting that guidance and developing a plan for implementation. The planner also, surprise, writes plans! From the small-scale site plan to neighborhood plans, to master plans for a city, or regional plans for a watershed or metropolitan area, planners analyze a range of transportation, social, economic, environmental, and cultural conditions or a place and design processes to engage and understand local interests and issues, then help to translate all of that into a series of goals and then the means to achieve those goals through new parks, rail, bike lanes, zoning, or other policies or programs.

Making the Case for Urban Design

The urban designer contributes to ensuring that a real estate development project positively impacts the broader context in which it is sited, as well as to create a high-quality public realm within the development (see Figure 8.2). Within the development, the design team has a lot of control, outside they must rely on a partnership with local government authorities.

Connecting the proposed new development with existing networks of sidewalks, trails, roads, public transit routes, and parks means a developer must converse with local government planners: here the urban designer can take the lead and develop ideas for those connections. An existing bus stop two blocks from the site border of a new development project might simply need the erection of wayfinding signage to make it easier for users of the new project to find the bus stop. A park down the hill from a new development could be extended through a vacant lot through a developer's modest donation to a local land trust

Figure 8.2   Plaza outside Union Station in Toronto, Canada. Justin B. Hollander.

so that this green space can reach the project boundaries and then continue onto the site, providing an amenity for the site's users, as well as the wider community.

These negotiations, brainstorming, and ideations are at the heart of the urban designer's job, building a development that does more than maximize profit, but builds mutual benefits with the host neighborhood and local government. While a real estate development firm may only seek to maximize profits, local government approvals may not be so easily obtained without a sense of these mutual benefits.

Scholars have studied this question for many years and largely concluded that for large-scale proposed development projects, this community buy-in is a requirement (Phillips and Pittman 2015). For smaller projects, a residential duplex, a 3,000 square foot retail stand-alone building, perhaps that larger urban design approach is not needed, but for anything bigger it appears to be a necessity.

The remainder of this chapter probes this mutual benefit more deeply, examining what precisely urban design can bring to a neighborhood or an entire community, and how do we measure this benefit.

The Science of Biometrics

The design fields are about to be completely remade and retrofitted because of the march of new knowledge being generated in scientific laboratories the world over. In 2012, the Organization of Economic Competitiveness and Development (OECD) framed recent history like this: the nineteenth century was the Age of Engineering, the twentieth century was the Age of Chemistry, and now, in the twenty-first century, we live in the Age of Biology. Unthinkable advanced in neuroscience, cognitive science, and evolutionary biology have given designers and planners a window into the human experience that were missing just a few decades back.

Today, we understand humans as fundamentally evolved mammals, bipedal, walking at approximately two miles per hour (Gehl 2010). Humans take in 11,000,000 bits of information into our brains every second, 10,000,000 bits are coming in through our eyes, and we are only processing around 50 bits consciously (Markowsky 2017). That means we are experiencing the world around us primarily unconsciously, whether the places around us make us happy, sad, healthy, or angry has little to do with our background or experience, age or gender, instead our responses to our environments are governed by preset patterns and traits that have been conserved through billions of years of evolution (Sussman and Hollander 2021).

Shortly after publishing the book *Cognitive Architecture*, we began to explore the tools of the psychologist and neuroscientist to better understand these patterns and traits – and most importantly, how planners and designers can best employ these insights to create places that work for that evolved mammal that we are, meandering about life largely on autopilot.

We began by measuring people's eye-movements when they looked at a building or streetscape. By honing in on the first 3–5 seconds, we can do something extraordinary: we can track the inner working of the human mind, we can map the ways that people see the world around them on an unconscious level. The results were astounding. Working first with the US Army, then the City of New York, and then the Devens Enterprise Commission, we generated remarkable results. We found that people fixated on buildings more in pedestrian-oriented urban environments than more car-centric places, that high-quality edges, buildings with face-like facades, and presence of greenery all impacted the movement and activity of peoples' eyes (Hollander et al. 2020). Continuing this research, we have done additional eye-tracking studies in four more cities and more recently began to use an eye-tracking emulation software tool to estimate how human eyes might look at an urban scene – without the need for bringing subjects into a laboratory (Hollander et al. 2021). The massive corporation, 3M, owns a product called Visual Attention Software (VAS), widely used in graphic design and marketing, but beginning to get some use in urban planning and design.

Early tests of VAS showed impressive insights, we could suddenly read a streetscape, understand the estimated time to first fixation, postulate the path a gaze might take across an image, and assess the strength of a place for welcoming viewing (all possible within seconds). Some of the most compelling research we have done in this vein has been comparing Da Nang, Vietnam with Boston, USA. That study demonstrated the power of historic buildings to connect with people's unconscious eye-movements so much better than modern buildings, across both cities. It suggests a new way of thinking about the nature of memory and historic preservation. Exciting research in neuroscience suggests that eye fixations are tied to memory, that the more we fixate and hold our eyes on an image (or a specific point on an image), the more we will retain that memory (Damiano and Walther 2019). Seeing it in action in these VAS images was simply startling, the memorable places in both cities were the ones that got the eye fixations in the VAS reports (see Figures 8.3–8.6).

Figure 8.3   Rockaway Beach. Justin B. Hollander and Ann Sussman.

Figure 8.4   Fordham Plaza. Justin B. Hollander and Ann Sussman.

Figure 8.5   Stapleton Plaza in New York original with eye-tracking. Justin B. Hollander and Ann Sussman.

Figure 8.6 Photoshopped Stapleton Plaza in New York with eye-tracking. Justin B. Hollander and Ann Sussman.

Urban Experience and Design

The discussion in Chapter 7 around Cognitive Architecture introduced a new way of looking at the design of buildings and landscapes. But this way of thinking can be even more profound as applied to urban design.

In the graphic design and computer science fields, there is a sub-discipline "user experience." Know in shorthand as Ux, its focus is on using the most advanced scientific research to design websites, brochures, equipment that is easy to use, intuitive, comfortable, and with low stress. Ergonomics is one area of Ux: the attention to how objects (chairs, keyboards, golf clubs) match our very human needs, easy to sit in, to grab, and to type at. What about applying these Ux concepts to the built environment?

The research reported above suggests that Ux does need to be applied to the built environment and such is the argument of a new book *Urban Experience and Design: Contemporary Perspectives on Improving the Public Realm* (Hollander and Sussman 2021). Using the shorthand, Ux+Design, the notion of user experience blends with urban experience in the birth of a new way for design and planning professionals to approach the shaping of the public realm.

Urban designers team up with architects, landscape architects, and urban planners to use biometrics and the latest insights from science to analyze and study how their proposed designs will shape the human experience before they build. The results (like those discussed earlier) center people in the development process, it becomes the human being, that evolved mammal, bipedal, walking at about two miles per hour, that becomes the organizing reference for the proposed project. This means stripping away dogma and theory, and focusing on what kind of environment does that human being need. The answers point back to the

Cognitive Architecture principles outlined in Chapter 7, but also stem from results gained from the kind of biometrics research described earlier. Does the design attract people to walk, does it put them at ease or make them stressed out, does it encourage them to socialize and congregate, and lastly, does it make them remember the place, make them want to come back again and again? If so, the development project will be successful beyond the short-term financial analysis, such results can be persuasive in arguing that the development can be a lasting, meaningful, and memorable part of a neighborhood and community's future. When time is money, a developer's need for a speedy review and approval of a project can hinge on just such questions. A focus on urban experience and design can give approval authorities the confidence that a proposed project will be mutually beneficial, for both the developer and the community.

Conclusion: Making the Case for Urban Planning

The local government planner can be a partner to a real estate developer or a nemesis. Both apolitical and politically savvy at the same time, the government planner can navigate the raw electoral needs of a mayor or city council with the aspirations of a community and the requirements of a real estate developer. When they succeed, everyone is friends, when they fail: enemies.

Much of the aim of this book has been to empower all players in the real estate development process to seek out ways for mutual gain, to look for the paths and pathways to responsible development. Neither the planner, nor the developer, nor any of the other professionals discussed here can do it alone; they must all be in sync with a common aim of doing more than pursuing profit. But if profit seeking is ignored, if the lessons from Chapters 3 and 4 are ignored, then real estate development will not end up being people-centered, it simply will not happen. Here, the urban planner has a critical role to play in balancing competing interests, understanding the big picture, and keeping the players on target toward responsible real estate development.

CASE STUDY: Gardner House

Project Background

Gardner House is a ninety-five-unit affordable apartment building developed by Mercy Housing Northwest, a non-profit affordable housing developer in Seattle, Washington (see Figure 8.7 and Table 8.1). Gardner House is targeted for families who have experienced homelessness or are at risk of homelessness (HUD's Office of Policy Development and Research 2020). The Paul G. Allen Family Foundation

Table 8.1 Gardner House, Seattle, Washington.

Location	Seattle, WA
Developer(s)	MHNW16 Family Housing LLP
Landowner(s)	Mercy Housing Northwest (non-profit)
Year Opened	February 2020
Housing Type	95 rental units
	• 28 units of permanent supportive housing for families needing intensive social services
	• 19 units are designated as "moving on" units and provide fewer intensive services to families in a more stable position
	• 47 units are reserved for families earning up to 60% AMI
	• 60% of units are two or three bedrooms
	• 10 units for large families
	• 2 units are designed to be licensed in-home childcare units for residents
People-centered Aspects	Mass transit access
	Evergreen Sustainable Development Standard certification
	Community-driven amenity
	Humble Design helped furnish apartments
	8,000-square-foot Allen Family Center (Child Care Resources, Mary's Place, and the Refugee Women's Alliance + food pantry)
People-centered Process	Urban design
Financing	• $30 million from the Paul G. Allen Family Foundation (a Microsoft founder)
	• $10 LIHTC
	• $5 million from the city of Seattle

(Allen was one of Microsoft's founders) contributed $30 million to the development and opened the 8,000-square-foot space on the first floor for non-profits (ibid). Gardner House is a transit-oriented development and is a block away from the Mount Baker light rail station, two blocks from the Metro transit center, and has its own bus stop (Van Streefkerk 2020) (see Figures 8.8 and 8.9). In regard to sustainability, Gardner House complies with Washington state's Evergreen Sustainable Development Standard certification and has rooftop solar panels, a storm-water retention system, and water- and energy-saving fixtures and appliances (HUD's Office of Policy Development and Research 2020). Gardner House also has a seven-story mural covering one of the building's sides.

Figure 8.7 Gardner House, Seattle, Washington. Nick Welch.

Figure 8.8 Close-up of Allen Family Center at Gardner House. Nick Welch.

Urban Design and Planning

Public realm is a major component of people-centered urban design and specific design choices like public art are appreciated by residents, neighbors, and visitors. At Gardner, the mural called "White Ashes" was created by Pacific Northwest

Figure 8.9 New bus stop in front of landscaped sidewalk outside Gardner House. Nick Welch.

Figure 8.10 Mural on Gardner House. Nick Welch.

artist, Kenji Hamai Stoll using aerosol and acrylic and encompasses seven of the eight stories of the building, measuring at 82' × 75' (Kenji Hamai Stoll n.d.) (see Figures 8.10 and 8.11). Further, Runberg, the architects behind the building, channeled the history of the Mount Baker neighborhood of Seattle and the gla- ciers' movements that defined the area by carving out spaces for residents that encourage light and air (Gardner House and Allen Family Center n.d.). While private and not open to the public, it is worth noting the second-floor courtyard

Figure 8.11 View of mural on Gardner House with laundromat out front. Nick Welch.

includes a playground funded by the Seattle Seahawks football team for the 100+ children who live in the building (Van Streefkerk 2020).

People-centered Components

In addition to the public realm elements that benefit the whole neighborhood, the community driven amenity, the Allen Family Center encompasses the first floor of the building and is home to the non-profits: Child Care Resources, Mary's Place, the Refugee Women's Alliance (ReWA), and a food pantry (Keller 2020). The center provides services for residents and the community at large. In terms of affordable housing, the Gardner House has 95 affordable units and are designed with families in mind. Over 60% of the units are two or three bedrooms and two units are specifically permitted to provide in-home childcare for residents (The Affordable Housing Tax Credit Coalition 2020). Access to the light rail stations and on-side bus stop, further enhances the people-centered nature of this development.

Case Takeaways

Unique community institutions and actors can make impacts at many different stages to enhance people-centered development, from large pecuniary gifts to normal aspects of childhood like play. I am sure quite a few children excitedly told their classmates about their Seattle Seahawks playground at their home. Further, people-centered urban design aspects such as the mural invite the public and community members to the development. Existing members of the community can and should help to shape people-centered development and the processes that underpin them.

Bibliography

Damiano, C. and Walther, D.B. (2019). Distinct roles of eye movements during memory encoding and retrieval. *Cognition* 184: 119–129. doi: 10.1016/j. cognition.2018.12.014.

Gardner House and Allen Family Center (n.d.). *Runberg Architecture Group*. http://runberg.com/work/gardner-house-and-allen-family-center (accessed January 18, 2022).

Gehl, J. (2010). *Cities for People*. Washington, DC: Island Press.

Hollander, J.B. and Sussman, A. (eds.) (2021). *Urban Experience and Design: Contemporary Perspectives on Improving the Public Realm*. New York and London: Routledge.

Hollander, J.B., Sussman, A., Lowitt, P. et al. (2021). Eye-tracking emulation software: a promising urban design tool. *Architectural Science Review* 64 (4): 383–393. doi: 10.1080/00038628.2021.1929055.

Hollander, J.B., Sussman, A., Purdy Levering, A. and Foster-Karim, C. (2020). Using eye-tracking to understand human responses to traditional neighborhood designs. *Planning Practice & Research* 35 (5): 485–509. doi: 10.1080/02697459.2020.1768332.

HUD's Office of Policy Development and Research (2020). Putting families first in the fight against homelessness. *The Edge, PD&R's Online Magazine*, November 16, 2020. https://www.huduser.gov/portal/pdredge/pdr-edge-inpractice-111620.html.

Keller, A. (2020). Luvissa and her family now have the Gardner House as a place to call their own. Vulcan (blog), 2020. https://vulcan.com/News/2020/Gardner-House.aspx.

Kenji Hamai Stoll (n.d.). *Kenji Hamai Stoll*. https://www.yokenji.net/recent (accessed April 5, 2022).

Markowsky, G. (2017). Information theory. *Encyclopædia Britannica, Inc.* https://www.britannica.com/science/information-theory.

Phillips, R. and Pittman, R. (2015). *An Introduction to Community Development*, 2e. New York and London: Routledge.

Sussman, A. and Hollander, J. (2021). *Cognitive Architecture: Designing for How We Respond to the Built Environment*, 2e. Routledge. doi: 10.4324/9781003031543.

The Affordable Housing Tax Credit Coalition (2020). *Gardner House in Seattle, WA, has won a 2020 Charles L. Edson Tax Credit Excellence Award in the Special Needs Category.* 2020. https://www.taxcreditcoalition.org/gallery/gardner-house.

Van Streefkerk, M. (2020). Mount Baker's Gardner House and Allen family center offer permanent housing and resources for underhoused families. *South Seattle Emerald (blog)*, June 26, 2020. https://southseattleemerald.com/2020/06/26/mount-bakers-gardner-house-and-allen-family-center-offer-permanent-housing-and-resources-for-underhoused-families.

9

Construction

Up until this point in the book, real estate development and planning have been introduced across the processes of site selection, analysis, and design. Now, we turn to the final official stage of any new development: construction. Along the continuum of policy/design activities introduced earlier in the book, construction is the most concrete, least abstract (see Figure 8.1). This is the point in the development process where foundations are dug, structures are erected, and land is graded. While architects and landscape architects will monitor construction, often maintaining a regular presence on site, they have metaphorically turned the keys over (along with their blueprints) to the construction professionals.

Those blueprints are in many ways an amazing thing. They express the ways that a development will overcome site constraints, respond to a site analysis, articulate a program of uses, and do it all in a way that enhances the experience of anyone who might be occupying or visiting the property. That enhanced experience can take numerous forms, but may come from employing cognitive architecture principles to make the buildings or landscape beautiful and welcoming or it may be a direct result of community input that helps the project meet the needs of residents.

But the blueprints are worthless if they just stay on paper (or a computer screen) (see Figures 9.1 and 9.2), it takes construction professionals to translate these designs into something three-dimensional, something real, something that will be safe, and something that will endure for years to come. Not an easy task.

There is a great need for architects, landscape architects, and urban designers and planners to really understand construction processes so that their blueprints can be translated to reality. We the authors have known numerous design professionals who have worked in the construction business as part of their training, helping to hammer nails, dig trenches, lay pipe, just to better understand this critical final stage.

Buildings for People: Responsible Real Estate Development and Planning, First Edition.
Justin B. Hollander and Nicole E. Stephens.
© 2023 John Wiley & Sons, Inc. Published 2023 by John Wiley & Sons, Inc.

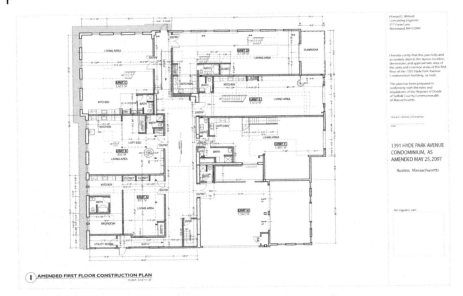

Figure 9.1 Floor plan drawn by architects: first floor of Hyde Park condominiums in Boston, Massachusetts. Phil Manker via Flickr, image has been cropped.

Figure 9.2 Example of exterior computer render of residential house.

This chapter seeks to provide a concise overview of what designers and planners need to know about construction in order to be able to do their jobs well. It also offers a summary of the construction business aimed at aspiring real estate developers. While the planner or designer plays an important role, they are not the first to act. It is the real estate developers that start the ball rolling for new projects and they need to know some basics about construction to ensure that they are starting off right.

The chapter begins by shifting all the way across the continuum diagram introduced in the last chapter (see Figure 8.1) to the most concrete of all topics: concrete. That is, materials and physical elements of construction, including the many tradespeople involved at each step. Next, we look closely at those materials and explore the range of rules and regulations in place that seek to achieve a variety of public benefits from construction. Lastly, we turn to the broader approaches that construction professionals take to their processes and discuss the ways that projects can be organized and structured.

Nothing more Concrete than Concrete

While the planner and developer might work out of climate-controlled offices, with indoor plumbing and kitchens, sometimes celebrating special occasions at hour-long lunches at spiffy sit-down restaurants. Construction professionals rough it a bit more. They operate out of mobile trailers and use port-a-potties, they grab lunch from their thermos or buy it off a food truck. For what is typically a long shift, construction workers remain isolated from surrounding amenities and endure a relatively dangerous work environment. At the top of any on-site operation will be a construction manager or project manager, overseeing all phases of a real estate development construction. These people will use Gantt charts or similar organizational systems to monitor and manage dozens or even hundreds of activities ranging from excavation, to fencing, to electrical, to plumbing (see Figure 9.3). A big project might have over 100 workers on a site at the same time, each doing their own job – but working together. The construction manager's job is then infinitely more complex than an orchestral conductor, but the analogy works – ensure that the building is framed, before the roofing team arrives, get the police to stop traffic, before the crane is needed on a local side street.

The range and number of different subcontractors, consultants, and in-house staff is astounding. We have personally been involved in a bathroom renovation recently and can testify that coordinating the schedules of the plumber and the electrician is exceptionally difficult: one wrong adjustment to the schedules and you just might risk getting electrocuted anytime someone flushes the toilet! How that actually works in a four-story apartment building project when there could be a dozen companies of over 100 workers all trying to work fluidly together is impressive.

The maestro (construction manager) then needs a staff of their own to organize and manage all of these moving parts in order to stay on time and under budget

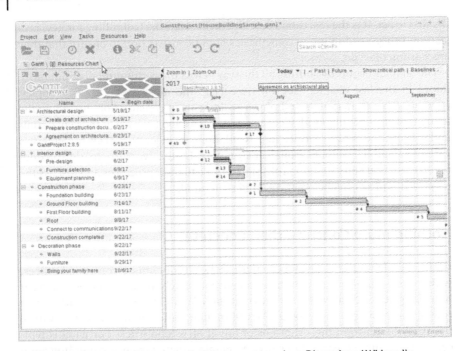

Figure 9.3 Gantt chart from sample development project. Dbarashev / Wkimedia Commons / CC BY-SA 4.0.

and meet key quality standards, without anyone getting hurt or anyone getting sued (Allen and Iano 2019). Did we mention the weather? Unknowns related to precipitation, high winds, and extreme heat or cold can also derail a construction manager's best laid plans.

The secret to success here is all about relationships. If the construction manager knows and trusts their team, they have nothing to fear. That means the selection of the various subcontractors and consultants is critical. Most medium and large construction projects are led by a general contractor (GC), who works directly for the developer (alternative models will be introduced later in the chapter). The GC appoints a construction manager to run the show for a given project, and then uses their own people (laborers and carpenters) as well as subcontractors and consultants, as needed. Key subcontractors will cover the major building systems like structural engineering, electrical, plumbing, HVAC (heating, ventilation, air conditioning), fire safety, and landscape.

Some basic nomenclature on buildings is useful here. Buildings can be constructed on slabs (generally concrete) or the earth can be excavated and a foundation built and the structure can rest on that foundation (see Figures

9.4–9.6). When the excavators go to work, it's hard to predict exactly what they will find so this stage of construction is rife with uncertainty. A notable example was when the US government was building a new federal office building in

Figure 9.4   Example of slab foundation. Bill Bradley / Wkimedia Commons / CC BY 2.5.

Figure 9.5   Basement foundation.

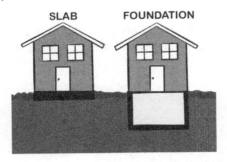

Figure 9.6 Diagram comparing slab and basement foundation. Diagram courtesy of Uma Edulbehram.

Lower Manhattan, New York City, they encountered skeletons. The site they had chosen turned out to be a burial ground for African slaves and free people, dating back almost 400 years (Frohne 2015). The real estate development team worked with archeologists and the construction group to redesign the building footprint and create the African Burial Ground National Monument at the site, an enduring memorial to the disturbed remains. A 30-plus story office tower was eventually built and currently houses a regional office of the US Environmental Protection Agency.

Turning back to construction materials, the vertical elements on a small structure can be framed in wood, but larger structures need masonry, concrete, or some form of metal framing (see Figures 9.7–9.10). Steel is considered very strong, durable, but expensive. Concrete is also pretty strong, cheap, but is subject to cracking. Wood is a strong material though it decomposes in time, degrading more quickly than steel or concrete. Then there is masonry, which is attractive as

Figure 9.7 Woodframe construction.

Figure 9.8 Masonry construction.

Figure 9.9 Concrete frame construction of skyscraper.

Figure 9.10 Steel and Concrete frame construction. Seth Whales / Wkipedia / CC BY-SA 4.0.

it is fire resistant and environmentally sound, though it is quite expensive as a material and expensive to install.

Once framed, most structures (except for some masonry buildings) need cladding to protect their framing. Cladding comes in the form of wood or plastic shingles, glass curtain walls, or metal or plastic siding (see Figures 9.11 and 9.12). These materials protect the building from the elements and are chosen based on local climatic conditions.

Figure 9.11 Glass curtain cladding.

Figure 9.12 Plywood cladding.

The building is topped off with a roof, again the exact shape and materials will be based on local conditions and a building's planned use. Sloped roofs are common is snowy regions, where a flat roof may be more appropriate in warmer environs and for warehouse structures. A roof can be constructed using asphalt, clay, metal, stone, or glass/plastic tiles, with each offering costs and benefits depending on the building's use, location, and time horizon. Stone slate roofs can last 100 years, but are expensive to install, while asphalt roofs are cheap but won't last more than a couple decades. Glass might seem an odd choice, but firms like Tesla are installing glass and plastic solar generating roof tiles on homes which also house their electric cars – providing an easy source of electricity to charge car batteries (Crail and Allen 2022).

One final point on materials: how they get to a construction site is more than a logistics question, it may figure into questions around site selection. A quirky location like a small island without a deep-water port clearly represents challenges around access to materials, but so does a site next to an elementary school (hundreds of tractor trailers dropping off bricks and steel over the course of weeks or months will generate massive air and noise pollution). If a project is sited near freight rail, materials can be transported less expensively than via truck. A small island is one thing, but a project site on the coast and adjacent to a deep-water port can receive materials via shipping containers, also cheap compared to truck deliveries.

Governing Construction

The public sector plays an extraordinary role in the construction process, regulating, controlling, and restricting buildings throughout all phases to promote a variety of goals, the primary one being safety. Most codes evolved is response to building collapses, fires, or other tragedies (Hall 1998). Building codes today are designed to reduce death and injury and powerful tool for local governments to protect public safety.

The architect needs to understand these building codes to develop their blueprints, how far columns should be spaced, what material should walls be made of, how tall should each building story be? But it is the construction professionals who have to understand these codes backward and forward in order to ensure that local authorities approve of their building. If a ramp is too steep or a hallway too narrow, a local government can force a builder to demolish and start anew (a very costly proposition).

In the United States, the International Building Code (IBC) is widely used by local governments, though others adopt popular regional or even home-grown codes – each distinct from one another. Construction professionals prefer the IBC because they know it and will seek out projects in locales that employ it. The IBC offers rules for different types of uses: industrial, public venues, residential, etc. For each, it also provides varying guidance for different construction types and hazard levels. The IBC is filled with numerous tables listing allowable heights and areas for these myriads of uses, densities, and types. Internationally, the IBC promotes cross-border construction activity to the extent that local governments adopt the code and construction firms bid beyond their home country – increasing competition and driving down construction costs.

Beyond building codes, the construction business is also constrained in the United States by federal laws that govern workplace safety (Occupational Safety and Health Act [OSHA]) and universal access (Americans with Disabilities Act [ADA]); other countries have similar such rules. Workplace safety rules are similar to building codes, but impose additional rules for construction professionals to abide by in both the construction process and in building office, industrial, or other workplaces. Like building codes, OSHA rules attempt to keep these places safe for workers by limiting exposure to toxins or poor air quality, requiring enhanced fire safety building systems, and maintaining high standards for elevators and other internal mobility systems in a new building, among other domains.

Universal access speaks to the ability of a person to enter and navigate a building, no matter their ambulatory condition, whether they walk, use a cane, or a wheelchair. These kinds of rules impose limits in constructing stairs, ramps, and steps, all aimed at making buildings fully accessible for all. In the United States, ADA requirements are fairly easy to meet in constructing new buildings, but more challenging in major renovations. Ultimately, there are costs to the construction process for all of the rules we are reviewing here, some costlier than others, but aside from changing the law or petitioning for a waiver most developers will work closely with their designers and construction team to find the most cost-effective ways to abide by these kinds of rules, sometimes curtailing other priorities in the process.

Local governments also have numerous other codes and regulations that they employ to direct and focus real estate developers to accomplishing public purposes with their projects. Below we will cover some environmental policies, but one common one is a priority for hiring local or union labor. It is uncommon for these kinds of policies to require such actions, but more likely that the city or town might offer incentives for developers to consider them.

Environmental Performance

There are a lot of reasons that construction professionals might care about the environmental performance of the materials they use and the buildings they build: buildings use about 65% of all electricity, 12% of potable water, and 30% of raw materials in the United States (Allen and Iano 2019 p. 6). In some localities, regulations actually require that construction project attain some level of environmental performance, in other situations companies are seeking to score well on broader measures of ESG (environmental, social, governance) ratings, or simply want a "green" building.

Just like with building codes, international and national organizations have developed standards to help construction professionals understand how their choices of materials and construction methods (and the overall design of a building) will impact environmental performance. The International Standard Organization (ISO) publishes standards across a broad spectrum of disciplines and their ISO 14020 specifically addresses green building materials.

ISO 14020 covers three types of standards relating to materials, the first Type I are ecolabels and cover third party certification of the environmental performance of a type of material. An example of a Type I certification system that complies with ISO 14020 is the Green Seal Standard. Green Seal is a non-profit organization that creates labeling standards for paints, cleaners, and packaging specifically restricting products from any hazardous ingredients like carcinogens. In hiring a painting subcontractor, a general contractor might note in their contract that all paints must be Green Seal certified.

Type II of ISO 14020 covers self-declared environmental claims by manufacturers, providing guidance for a company which wants to tout the environmental performance of its products. Type III standards deal with environmental impact labels that are independently verified, which might speak to the life-cycle impact of a bathroom tile or glass pane. A notable example is the Western Red Cedar Association's declaration that for every 100 square feet of its decking, 2.5 million BTU of energy is used and 0.1 gallon of water is consumed – impressive figures when compared with competitors (Allen and Iano 2019).

In the United States, the US Green Building Council runs the Leadership in Environmental and Energy Design (LEED) program that foremost certifies construction projects as "green" at different performance levels, certified, silver, green, and platinum (Figure 9.13). LEED covers materials, but also siting, construction methods and techniques, and other energy efficiency and environmental dimensions of development. Some local governments have adopted these LEED standards in their development regulations, requiring certain large construction projects to attain a given LEED rating.

Figure 9.13 Soldier Field Stadium in Chicago, Illinois, the first LEED certified NFL stadium. Ken Lund / Flickr / CC BY-SA 2.0.

The Construction Process

The construction manager might run a construction process, but how that process is designed needs to be set by the real estate developer. There are a few of these processes, otherwise known as project delivery methods: design/bid/build, design/build, turnkey, or single-purpose entity (Allen and Iano 2019; Sears, et al. 2015). Under design/bid/build, a real estate developer hires a design team (architects, landscape architects, urban designs, engineers) that writes up not only the blueprints, but a more detailed request for proposals document that is put out to bid. General contractors then respond to that bid with their price, qualifications, and schedule and the developer selects the bid that best meets their needs. This sequential approach is the most common one and is one generally preferred by non-profit or government developers due to its transparency.

A faster and more efficient approach is design/build where the developer just hires one company that will both design and build a project. The single step means fewer checks or time for quality control in the design process, the single firm is trusted to simply deliver on the program and to coordinate internally as necessary. On the flip side, the ability of architects and contractors to communicate seamlessly within a single design/build company can reduce the likelihood of errors or mistakes.

Less common is when a builder does it all, the turnkey approach is helper for a real estate developer without experience (or interest in gaining experience) like a university or hospital. They hire a builder to run the whole project, from financing, the public sector engagement, from designers to engineers to plumbers. Similarly, is the single-purpose entity, where the real estate developer has all those talents in-house and doesn't hire anyone – here a company with experience in managing apartment buildings (and extensive in-house expertise around marketing, financing, construction, and politics) might just handle an entire real estate development project solo.

Conclusion

The construction process is at the end of any real estate development, but needs to be considered throughout all stages. The materials, trades, environmental performance, governance role, and project deliver methods are all critical considerations for a real estate developer. Investments in the right areas at the right time can make the difference between a safe, high quality, comfortable building and one that is not.

Below we turn to our final case study, illustrating some of the ideas presented in this chapter.

CASE STUDY: A.O. Flats at Forest Hills

Table 9.1 A.O. Flats at Forest Hills, Boston, Massachusetts.

Location	Boston, MA
	Jamaica Plain neighborhood
Developer(s)	The Community Builders (non-profit)
Landowner(s)	Urbanica (private)
Year Opened	Fall 2020
Housing Type	78 income-restricted rental units
	• 30 workforce housing units up to 120% AMI
	• 40 affordable units at no more than 60% AMI
	• 8 for formerly homeless families at 30% AMI
	8 studios
	37 one-bedroom units
	25 two-bedroom family units
	8 three-bedroom family units
People-centered Components	• Non-luxury housing
	• Public transit access
	• Pocket Park
Process Highlighted	Construction
Financing	• $2.25 million in the Department of Neighborhood Development funding (City of Boston)
	• $750,000 in Neighborhood Housing Trust Funds (City of Boston)
	• $8.1 million in Mass Housing Workforce funding (Commonwealth of Massachusetts)
	• $13.09 million Mass Housing permanent funding (Commonwealth of Massachusetts)
	• $8.84 million in Equity (Low-Income Housing Tax Credit and Solar) (Federal)
	• $2.6 million sponsor loan from The Community Builders (non-profit)

Project Background

Jamaica Plain (JP) is a populous neighborhood in Boston southwest of the downtown core. It is home to Jamaica Pond, Arnold Arboretum, and Sam Adams Brewery and is serviced by four stops on the MBTA's Orange Line branch.

According to the City of Boston, the population of JP grew 9% between 2000 and 2015 to 39,240 and occupied housing units increased by 12% (Boston Planning & Development Agency Research Division 2017). JP, like most of Boston, struggles with maintaining and building affordable housing for current and new residents. The Massachusetts Bay Transit Authority (MBTA) is a large landholder in the area and is actively pursuing opportunities to expand transit-oriented development.

The firm Urbanica was chosen as the developer for a large "Parcel U" project by the MBTA for development adjacent to train tracks. The Parcel U development was broken into smaller phases and phase "C" was a five-story mixed-income rental building. Called A.O. Flats (see Figure 9.14 and Table 9.1), Urbanica partnered with The Community Builders (TCB) a non-profit that began in Boston's South End but has since grown to operate nationally as the primary developer for the mixed-income building (Urbanica 2014 p. 40). A.O. Flats sits (see Figures 9.15–9.17) on about a third of the 2.8-acre Parcel U site, which was sold to Urbanica for roughly a million dollars in 2013 (MBTA 2008; MBTA Realty n.d.). A.O. Flats is a transit-oriented development with both underground and on-street parking as well as bike storage with one bike space per unit (Kimura 2021).

Construction

The site was fully excavated and an underground garage was installed below-grade, featuring 42 parking spaces. Steel and concrete were used to build the

Figure 9.14   Street view of A.O Flats at Forest Hills in Boston. Courtesy of Uma Edulbehram.

Figure 9.15 Close-up street view of A.O. Flats. Courtesy of Uma Edulbehram.

Figure 9.16 Street view of A.O. Flats. Courtesy of Uma Edulbehram.

foundation and the structures were framed in wood, flat roofs, with walls clad in plastic siding. During the construction phase, Urbanica employed people-centered ideas through its intentional hiring practices. Urbanica was a single-purpose entity, it was the designer, developer, and constructor for A.O. Flats and the larger Parcel U development, fully controlling the hiring process throughout.

Figure 9.17 A.O. Flats and access to public transportation. Courtesy of Uma Edulbehram.

During the construction process, Urbanica employed roughly 250 people (A.O. Flats Housing Development Opens at Forest Hills 2020) and an estimated 38% of construction contract value went to Minority Business Enterprise firms and 13% to Women Business Enterprise firms (Jack Kemp Excellence in Affordable and Workforce Housing Awards 2021 Winner: A.O. Flats at Forest Hills 2021). The full Parcel U development project was a pilot program with MassDOT/MBTA Diversity Development Program (MBTA Realty, n.d.). Urbanica intentionally selected underserved communities to benefit in the construction of A.O. Flats.

Urbanica made extra efforts to create a green building, earning A.O. Flats the LEED Platinum certification. The project features high-efficiency heating and cooling systems, Energy Star rated appliances and materials, and PV (photovoltaic) solar panels (A.O. Flats Housing Development Opens at Forest Hills 2020), all environmentally sustainable elements that benefit current and future residents.

People-centered Components

A.O. flats people-centered components included affordable housing, access to public transportation, and public outdoor space. In terms of affordable housing, A.O. Flats exceeds Boston's required affordability component in new developments, which currently requires that 13% be set aside as income-restricted (Boston Planning & Development Agency 2019). With A.O. Flats, 100% of the 78 rental units are income-restricted with 51% of the units reserved for low-income individuals and families with an additional eight set aside for the formerly homeless (Department of Neighborhood Development 2019). Referrals for the latter units are made through HomeStart, which manages Boston's Homeless Set Aside

Program (Boston HSA n.d.). The remaining thirty rental units are capped at 120% area median income (AMI), which is roughly considered to be workforce level housing in Boston. The affordable housing component of the development services multiple income levels including the most vulnerable.

The full development parcel contains three pocket parks (see Figures 9.18), the largest and public one is adjacent to A.O. Flats. Each pocket park has a distinct landscape such as a forest or meadow, with the park adjacent to the A.O. Flats created as a natural playground (Urbanica 2014 p .116). By being open to the public, the amenity integrates the new development into the existing community and invites neighbors to the space.

Case Takeaways

Government owned or previously owned land parcels provide a unique opportunity for people-centered developments. The MBTA sold the land to Urbanica for a modest sum ($1 million) with the explicit requirements that their development meet a certain affordability threshold. This case demonstrates how government entities through their public land holdings can prioritize things other than profit maximization in development, a common theme within the cases that we explored in this book. This case also demonstrates how developers can also align their processes to make them more people-centered. By hiring minority construction firms, the construction phase actively supports hiring and job creation that benefits the surrounding neighborhood.

Figure 9.18 Instance of pocket park adjacent to A.O. Flats. Courtesy of Uma Edulbehram.

Bibliography

Allen, E. and Iano, J. (2019). *Fundamentals of Building Construction: Materials and Methods*. New York: John Wiley & Sons.

A.O. Flats Housing Development Opens at Forest Hills (2020). *Boston.Gov* (blog). September 17, 2020. https://www.boston.gov/news/ao-flats-housing-development -opens-forest-hills.

Boston HSA (n.d.) Home Start. https://www.homestart.org (accessed July 10, 2022).

Boston Planning & Development Agency (2019). A.O. Flats. http://www.bostonplans. org/housing/income,-asset,-and-price-limits (Accessed February 12, 2022a).

Boston Planning & Development Agency Research Division (2017). *Neighborhood Profile: Jamaica Plain*. June 2017. http://www.bostonplans.org/ getattachment/45b73b74-dd3d-41cb-9cc6-40aa2e7cd009 (accessed July 10, 2022).

Clough, R.H., Sears, G.A., and Keoki Sears, S. (2000). *Construction Project Management*. New York: Wiley.

Clough, R.H., Sears, G.A., Keoki Sears, S. et al. (2015). *Construction Contracting: A Practical Guide to Company Management*. Hoboken, New Jersey: John Wiley And Sons.

Crail, C. and Allen, S. (2022). *How much does a tesla solar roof cost?* [online] *Forbes Home*. https://www.forbes.com/home-improvement/solar/tesla-solar-roof-cost (accessed July 11, 2022).

Department of Neighborhood Development (2019). *Affordable/Income-Restricted Rental Opportunity*. https://www.boston.gov/sites/default/files/imce-uploads/2019-06/ ao_flats_parcel_u_bfhc_approved_compliance_1_-_ads_outreach_1.pdf.

Frohne, A.E. (2015). *The African Burial Ground in New York City*. Syracuse University Press.

Hall, P. (1998). *Cities of Tomorrow: An Intellectual History of Urban Planning and Design Since 1880*. New York: John Wiley & Sons.

Jack Kemp Excellence in Affordable and Workforce Housing Awards 2021: Winnder: A.O. Flats at Forest Hills (2021). ULI Americas. https://americas.uli.org/programs/ awards-competitions/jack-kemp-awards (accessed April 17, 2022).

Kimura, D. (2021). Boston mixed-income development bolsters community. *Multifamily Executive*, September 14, 2021.

MBTA (2008). *Forest Hills MBTA DRAFT Invitation to Bid*. BPDA (formerly the BRA). http://www.bostonplans.org/documents/planning/downtown-neighborhood- planning/forest-hills-improvement-initiative/forest-hills-mbta-draft-invitation-to- bid (accessed July 11, 2022).

MBTA Realty (n.d.) *Under Construction 'Parcel U, Forest Hills'*. https://www. mbtarealty.com/wp-content/uploads/projects/1278/Parcel-U.pdf (accessed July 10, 2022).

Ortiz, P. (2013). *The Art of Shaping the Metropolis*. McGraw Hill Professional.

Ritz, G.J. and Levy, S.M. (2013). *Total Construction Project Management*. New York Mcgraw Hill Professional.

Sears, S.K., Sears, G.A., Clough, R.H., Rounds, J.L., and Segner, R.O. (2015). *Construction Project Management*. New York: John Wiley & Sons.

Urbanica (2014). *Parcel U Expanded Project Notification Form (PNF)*. BPDA (formerly the BRA). http://www.bostonplans.org/documents/projects/development-project-filings/parcel-u-pnf-2014-08-04 (accessed July 10, 2022).

10

Conclusion

Through these pages, we have offered a sweeping overview of the real estate development and planning process. Through a framing of responsible real estate development and the inclusion of five exemplary cases, we have argued that the building and shaping of human settlements can serve a number of public and private objectives. Responsible real estate development means that affordability, community-driven amenities, sustainability, access to public transportation, and meaningful public spaces become centered in a project right up alongside profit. Here, the lessons of Chapter 3 around financial analysis and running a pro forma become so important: the profit motive is still there and is still critical. When investors are not able to generate sufficient income to cover the costs of their investment, they reduce those costs to ensure a profitable return for themselves. Investors cut costs which lead to infrastructure negligence, client displacement, and negative impacts to the community appearance and social structure.

Even non-profit organizations are bound by their own finite resources, the costs of borrowing, and the potential rents they might collect. The profit (or in the case of a non-profit organization, the ability of a real estate development project to be financially realistic) matters and needs to be considered at each of the stages of the development process outlined here: site selection, site analysis, architecture/landscape architecture, urban design/planning, and construction. If decisions made at any of these stages compromise the ability to secure financing or limit potential future income, then a project dies (at quite a high cost, depending on the stage). No real estate developer wants that to happen; instead they seek out projects, sites, programs, local government partners, and development teams that can see a project through the completion and do it in a way that works financially. But achieving completion and profit is not what this book is about. We are calling out a responsible real estate development path where those community components

Buildings for People: Responsible Real Estate Development and Planning, First Edition.
Justin B. Hollander and Nicole E. Stephens.
© 2023 John Wiley & Sons, Inc. Published 2023 by John Wiley & Sons, Inc.

are prioritized. First: address the needs of people in a community, invest in infrastructure that will support disadvantaged populations, keep housing costs down for residential projects, and create public spaces that enhance places for people. For a project to be responsible, it does all of those things and also attends to profit – it does both and it gets done.

One project that truly exemplifies responsible real estate development is Plaza Roberto Maestas (Chapter 6). The developers, El Centro de la Raza and Beacon Development Group, addressed the needs of the community in the Northern Seattle area by creating a multifaceted development that incorporated transit accessibility, community engagement, and a public, civic gathering space. In order to successfully develop this project, the developers had to plan based on their resources, limits, and neighborhood support. Coordinated with a focus on the people, from the developers including a childcare center to them engaging with surrounding community to garner support, Plaza Roberto Maestas used a people centered site analysis and planning process that checks all of the boxes off of responsible real estate developments.

In Chapter 9, we introduced the idea that real estate development projects can be rated based on their environmental, social, or governance (ESG) performance. This framework is most widely embraced at the construction stage to ensure that a project has a low environmental impact in both its construction and operation. But entire companies are also evaluated through several independent organizations and rated on more than just how well they recycle construction debris, but also how diverse their corporate boards are and how well they support the communities they work in. These ESG ratings are an increasingly important dimension of business success and are a critical measure in evaluating how responsible a real estate project (or string of projects) might be (Cajias et al. 2014; Wong et al. 2021).

Because customers, investors, and rating agencies are looking at a company's ESG score in addition to their financials, real estate developers need to take seriously the lessons contained here in this book. Pursuing profit is great, but ignoring people, despoiling the environment, disrupting community well-being, these can all translate directly into lower ESG scores and doom a real estate development company's future plans.

As illustrated in the A.O. Flats at Forest Hills case study in Chapter 9, construction is something that should be considered throughout the entire process of real estate development even though it only happens at the end. Including people-centered principles throughout the construction process led to affordable housing, transportation accessibility, and a beneficial hiring and job creation process that targeted minority construction firms. The construction process solidifies that environmental, social, governance performance, and project delivery methods are critical components to the real estate developer and to the projected success of the project.

A related and growing field within ESG is impact investing. Here, a fund seeks out investment projects which promise a reasonable financial return but more importantly a wallop of a social or environmental return (Vecchi et al. 2017; Agrawal and Hockerts 2021). In the impact investing world, real estate development projects are attractive for financing and if done in a responsible fashion, can deliver both returns and impact for the impact investor. Developers can tap these impact investing funds as part of a mix of sources, but only if their work aligns with the investor – which will typically require many of the elements outlined here in this book: affordable housing, community infrastructure, sustainability, transit access, and an improved public realm.

Final Thoughts

Responsible and people-centered real estate development means doing business differently than the status quo. Any time innovators go beyond the ordinary, barriers appear. In this book, we are seeking to educate and enlighten and, in the process, remove some barriers and show what really is possible. The cases presented point to the power of creative, passionate people, engaged and effective government agencies, and committed and mission-driven non-profit actors in mitigating and managing those hurdles to achieve award-winning outcomes for themselves and their communities.

In reviewing the literature in the first two chapters of this book, we emphasized public land, sustainability, government funding, and the role of non-profits. These concepts were explored more deeply in the case studies through affordable housing, community-based amenities, transit access, and public outdoor space as components in the developments. The projects we reviewed also made some of the typical real estate development processes more people-centered by their intentionality in hiring, design, and community involvement.

The power of government policy and funding in creating people-centered development through development, land-use, and profit is clear in both the literature and cases reviewed. Local governments ought to expand program access and funding for people-centered development components and processes. Incentivizing people-centered practices through funding and other incentives like added density offers developers a carrot. The literature and these cases point to the power of the federal government in setting larger policy goals, such as providing for military family and defense worker housing, and the power of state and local governments in creating programs and acting entrepreneurially to solve problems.

Just as governments can encourage certain outcomes, they can also disincentivize development practices that it would like to be phased out – a stick. Taxes and fees are the most common versions of this, such as Boston's proposed flipping tax, which would tax properties valued at over $2 million that are sold multiple times within two years. A powerful argument against this localized tax though, is that developers will simply build elsewhere.

Both people-centered development components and processes can and should be incorporated into development projects by both real estate professionals and planners. Many non-profits are already people oriented and can help profit-motivated developers expand their practice. Governments at all levels can further incentivize people-centered practices through innovative policies and funding, changing the culture of land development to focus on community and people needs, in addition to the profitability imperative.

Bibliography

Agrawal, A. and Hockerts, K. (2021). Impact investing: review and research agenda. *Journal of Small Business & Entrepreneurship* [online] 33 (2): 153–181. Available at: https://www.semanticscholar.org/paper/Impact-investing%3A-review-and-research-agenda-Agrawal-Hockerts/8aa3feb96e665a88442f4d162f2e6bc033a2d481 (Accessed November 8, 2022).

Cajias, M., Fuerst, F., McAllister, P., and Nanda, A. (2014). Do responsible real estate companies outperform their peers? *International Journal of Strategic Property Management* 18 (1): 11–27. doi: 10.3846/1648715x.2013.866601.

Vecchi, V., Balbo, L., Brusoni, M., and Caselli, S. (2017). *Principles and Practice of Impact Investing A Catalytic Revolution*. Routledge.

Wong, W.C., Batten, J.A., Ahmad, A.H. et al. (2021). Does ESG certification add firm value? *Finance Research Letters* 39: 101593. doi: 10.1016/j.frl.2020.101593.

Appendix

Notes on Case Study Methods

To provide examples for the chapters in this book, we utilized the case study method, specifically a holistic multi-unit analysis, to research recent development projects in North America that are people-centered (Yin 1994). How did we determine what is people-centered? Based on our findings from reviewing the literature on alternative models in Chapter 2, we see people-centered development as development in which profit is not the primary motivator. Additionally, as we drew together the cases, we identified people-centered components like affordable housing, community-driven amenities, access to public transportation, and outdoor public space across the developments we reviewed.

To find examples of people-centered developments, we examined the Urban Land Institute's Jack Kemp Excellence in Affordable and Workforce Housing award and compiled an initial list of twenty potential case studies from their list of finalists and winners from 2015–2021. Established in 2008, the award honors developments that expand housing opportunities for people at a variety of income levels and requires that the developments meet certain thresholds of affordability, such as 50% of the affordable units be for households making less than 60% AMI (Jack Kemp Excellence in Affordable and Workforce Housing Awards n.d.). In 2022 the award was split into two awards: one for affordable housing and a second for middle-income housing (ibid). From the initial list of winners and finalists, we narrowed it to five developments to use as examples of people-centered developments for this book (see Table A.1). Given the nature of the award, affordable housing is a major component of all these developments, but other characteristics vary. Of the five chosen cases all are in large cities: two are in Boston, Massachusetts; two are in Seattle, Washington; and one is in Denver, Colorado.

We currently live and work in Boston and have so for more many years. We are familiar with the identified developments and the neighborhoods they are in. One of the authors, Nicole, attended high school in Seattle in the mid-2000s and maintain close ties with people in that city and continue to follow development there.

Buildings for People: Responsible Real Estate Development and Planning, First Edition.
Justin B. Hollander and Nicole E. Stephens.
© 2023 John Wiley & Sons, Inc. Published 2023 by John Wiley & Sons, Inc.

Table A.1 Overview of selected people-centered developments (by Nicole Stephens).

Development Name	Gardner House	A.O. Flats at Forest Hills	Plaza Roberto Maestas	Mosaic on the Riverway	Arroyo Village
ULI's Jack Kemp Award	Finalist, 2021	Winner, 2021	Winner, 2019	Winner, 2017	Winner, 2020
Landowner	Mercy Housing Northwest	Urbanica	El Centro de la Raza	Massachusetts' Department of Mental Health	Rocky Mountain Communities; The Delores Project
Developer	Mercy Housing Northwest	The Community Builders	El Centro de la Raza	Roxbury Tenants of Harvard	Rocky Mountain Communities; The Delores Project
Outdoor Public Space		Three Pocket Parks	Central Plaza	Playground	
Access to Public Transportation	Yes	Yes	Yes	Yes	Yes
Community Driven Amenity	Allen Family Center		Cultural Center; Early Childhood Center	Childcare Center	Shelter for Women and Transgender Individuals
Affordable Housing	95 rental units	78 rental units	112 rental units	60 rental; 43 condos	60 rental; 43 condos
Neighborhood	Mount Baker	Jamaica Plain	Beacon Hill	Longwood Medical Area	West Denver
City	Seattle, WA	Boston, MA	Seattle, WA	Boston, MA	Denver, CO
Year Opened	2020	2020	2019	2016	2019

We did not bring any substantial pre-existing knowledge or experience to the Denver case, though we have both visited the city.

For the cases we selected, we completed a document review of government publication and documentation submitted for public meeting like site plans, pro forma, and various contracts, non-profit reports, newspapers (both city-wide and smaller neighborhood weeklies), local blogs, public radio reports, and websites about the developments. Each case analysis includes a table with details on the development and characteristics like location, developer, landowner, year opened, housing type, other spaces, and finances. We also include in the table the projects' people-centered components and a development process (site selection, urban design, etc.); but, for each of the cases we describe how unique people-centered values were incorporated into a standard development process (see Table A.2). In addition to the table introducing each development, we have also included photos and plans of the development and a detailed narrative on the project background, specific process highlighted, people-centered components, and takeaways for each case, embedded in each chapter.

To aid the reader in better understanding the affordable housing components of each case study, we created a table comparing the area median income (AMI) in Boston, Seattle, and Denver for 2021 (see Table A.3). AMI is used to determine if a person is eligible to receive housing assistance, and it is based on income and household size. Compiled annually, it is region-specific and housing programs and units are set at different percentages. Of the three cities, Boston has the highest AMI followed by Seattle and then Denver.

The average area income, what most people or households make in each city annually, is 100% AMI. Affordable housing programs targeted for low-income people tend to be at the 30%–60% AMI level, such as the federally distributed low-income housing tax credits (LIHTC) and section 8 vouchers. Affordable

Table A.2 Development processes (by Nicole Stephens).

Process highlighted	Making it people-centered
Site selection	Community engagement drives the site selection and what the development will be
Site analysis and planning	After site selection, how factors that are typically viewed as constraints become opportunities for the development
Landscape/architecture	Intentional design decisions for the population served
Urban design	Public realm and public facing aspects of the development
Construction	Intentional hiring decisions with who is building the development

Table A.3 Comparison of AMI across case study cities (by Nicole Stephens).

		Area Median Income (AMI)2021				
			Low income		*Average area income*	
		30% AMI	50% AMI	60% AMI	100% AMI	120%AMI
Boston						
	1 person household	$ 25,400	$ 42,300	$ 50,750	$ 84,600	$ 101,500
	4 person household	$ 36,250	$ 60,400	$ 72,500	$ 120,800	$ 144,950
Seattle						
	1 person household	$ 24,300	$ 40,500	$ 48,590	$ 80,990	$ 97,190
	4 person household	$ 34,700	$ 57,850	$ 69,400	$ 115,700	$ 138,840
Denver						
	1 person household	$ 22,050	$ 36,700	$ 44,016	$ 73,360	$ 88,032
	4 person household	$ 31,450	$ 52,400	$ 62,880	$ 104,800	$ 125,760

ownership programs are newer interventions and tend to be state- or city-funded and are targeted at people making 100% AMI or greater. If a city or state is funding the affordable housing component, they can choose what AMI level to target.

Throughout this book, we encourage the reader to review these tables and consider the similarities and differences across the cases. Important lessons are offered through these about both the overall real estate development and planning process and what it means for actors to be responsible and people-centered.

References

Yin, R.K. (1994). *Case Study Research: Design and Methods*. New York: Sage.
Jack Kemp Excellence in Affordable and Workforce Housing Awards (n.d.) ULI Americas. https://americas.uli.org/programs/awards-competitions/jack-kemp-awards (accessed April 17, 2022).

Index

Buildings for People: Responsible Real Estate Development and Planning, First Edition.
Justin B. Hollander and Nicole E. Stephens.
© 2023 John Wiley & Sons, Inc. Published 2023 by John Wiley & Sons, Inc.

Printed and bound by CPI Group (UK) Ltd, Croydon, CR0 4YY

16/06/2023

03227636-0001